FOREIGN POLICY
AND THE
AMERICAN DEMOCRATIC
SYSTEM

PACEM IN TERRIS IV

Volume I
American-Soviet Detente,
Peace and
National Security

Volume II
American Foreign Policy
and The Third World

Volume III
Foreign Policy and The
American Democratic System

Foreign Policy and The American Democratic System

Edited by
Fred Warner Neal

Volume III of three volumes edited from the proceedings of
PACEM IN TERRIS IV
A National Convocation to Consider the Issues
in U.S. Foreign Policy in the Bicentennial Year,
Convened in Washington, D.C., December 2-4, 1975 by
The Fund for Peace
and
The Center for the Study of Democratic Institutions

Pacem in Terris IV
Box 4446
Santa Barbara, California 93103

Library of Congress Catalog Card Number: 74-78887
ISBN Cloth Set 0-87182-100-1
ISBN Cloth Vol. III 0-87182-103-6
ISBN Paper Set 0-87182-105-2
ISBN Paper Vol. III 0-87182-108-7

Printed in the United States of America

Acknowledgments

The Fund for Peace and the Center for the Study of Democratic Institutions gratefully acknowledge the generosity of the more than 5,000 of their supporters whose grants and donations and attendance made *Pacem in Terris IV* possible.

Robert M. Hutchins
Randolph P. Compton
Co-Chairmen

Contents

REFERENCE MATTER

Introduction:

The Cold War, Detente
and
Our Domestic Malaise

For more than twenty-five years, the Cold War dominated the United States. It produced a psychology and a culture of its own, with fear of and hostility toward the Soviet Union and communism as the main motif. And it produced a morality of its own, which justified any means in the name of combatting these perceived threats. The relation of all this to what has happened within the United States during these years is close and direct.

The Cold War orientation, more than any other factor, has been responsible for distortion of our constitutional process, the disastrous performance of our economy, the assault on our civil liberties, the moral corruption in government and the widespread public cynicism and apathy which characterize the American scene in the 1970s. And if one looks at the purely foreign policy results —whether in terms of national security, stemming the development of communism, competing for influence with the U.S.S.R., or military success—the results are not very reassuring either. To paraphrase the Duke of Wellington, our Cold War stance may not have frightened the enemy, but by God, sir, it should frighten us.

It is illustrative of the hold that the Cold War psychology has on us that those who deplore these domestic conditions seldom relate them directly to the Cold War foreign policy and even less often relate them to the groping efforts made in recent years to escape from it via a detente relationship with the Soviet Union. We are out of one phase of the Cold War, but it is far from certain that we will achieve a modus vivendi with the U.S.S.R. that will finally free us from the devastating effects of Cold War politics. If we do fail to achieve it, we are quite likely to continue to have the Cold War with us in greater or lesser degree. And if this should be the case, it is difficult to see how we can work our way out of the domestic malaise which grips us.

Consider the main subjects taken up in this third volume of the *Pacem in Terris IV* series. First there are the depredations committed by the CIA. In an eloquent statement, Senator Frank Church lists the almost un-believable series of secret and often illegal actions carried out at home and abroad by the intelligence agency—many of them fortunately bungled and therefore unsuccessful—and he does make the connection between these activities anti-communist obsession of the Cold War. He thinks that adequate legislative restraints and congressional oversights will guard against a repetition of CIA abuses. Even William Colby, then director of the CIA, agrees that such restraints and oversights are needed.

On the other hand, one can make a good case that it is not the lack of legal restraints and oversights which resulted in CIA's nefarious record. Indeed, one can make a case that neither the CIA as an organization nor the individuals comprising it is basically at fault. The trouble was the Cold War *zeitgeist* in which it operated. There are few acts for which the CIA is now being so widely criti-cized that either did not have or would not have had—if everything had been known—approval by the Congress and probably by a majority of the voters; and even fewer where CIA activities did not have the imprimatur of the White House and its minions.

And it was not only the CIA. The FBI's violations of constitutional guarantees are in one way more dangerous domestically, and the Pentagon's chicanery worse abroad. The whole executive branch of the government has been involved—with Congress usually cheering them on.

Congress for the moment, in a period of relatively easy relations with Moscow, sounds different and in certain instances has acted differently. There are daily proclamations from Capitol Hill about how Congress is going to insist on its prerogatives and redress the imbalance which executive excesses have wrought. The point, however, is not so much that activities like those for which the CIA is now being criticized should not be undertaken without congressional approval as it is that they should not be undertaken at all. Congress, throughout the whole post-war period, has been a weak reed to lean on. How long will the new mood continue if American-Soviet relations go sour again? And if they do, will we not be back in the same situation, where anything goes in the name of anti-communism and national security? The reaction of the Ford Administration to the congressional ban on further intervention in Angola is an indication of the pressures Congress ill be under.

In the second part of this volume, several distinguished experts, led by Mayor Tom Bradley of Los Angeles, deplore the effects of military spending on the domestic economy, especially as it contributes to the plight of our cities and to that economic miracle in reverse, high unemployment with high inflation. Professor Seymour Melman pinpoints the relationship with an impressive array of data. It is quite clear that if government action is to be undertaken to meet dire human needs in the country without heating up the inflation still more, it can be financed only by reducing the military budget. Yet even now, with the Cold War in a soft stage, the military budget goes up. If the Cold War atmosphere hardens, can there be doubts that it will rise even more precipitously?

The point is made in this book that national security in the military sense is meaningless without good public morale, that it is undermined by disaffected youth and minorities, long lines of unemployed and a distrustful populace reeling under constantly soaring prices and taxes. It is impossible to argue the point. And it is clear that if we are engaged in a global competition with communism, an asset even stronger than multi-overkill in nuclear weapons is a system that works for the benefit of its people. Yet short of laying the Cold War—and the Cold War psychology—to rest once and for all, how are we going to face up to these problems squarely, let alone solve them?

These omens are scarcely encouraging. But the third part of the present volume is in some ways the most frightening of all. The participating congressional leaders present some significant and innovative proposals. But they tend to feel there is little public interest in the foreign policy aspects of the issues cited above and that these are unlikely to be raised in a meaningful way during the 1976 campaign. In other words, the people are apathetic and those aspiring to leadership will not risk trying to guide them.

Senator Howard Baker dissents from this evaluation, putting his faith in the "collective genius of the American people" and the American political system to come up with the right answers. He could be right. We seem to be at some sort of turning point. But for a nation—even one with a collective genius—to turn in the right direction requires both public understanding of the issues and leadership to marshal its human and material resources. The *Pacem in Terris IV* Convocation was an effort to help provide the understanding as far as foreign policy is concerned. The whereabouts of the leadership is something else, however. The three volumes resulting from the Convocation could well be used as a primer for American voters wishing to explore all sides of these complicated problems. And if it helps them in choosing the right leaders—or even in deciding whom not to choose—the effort will not have been altogether in vain.

Fred Warner Neal

Claremont
March, 1976

I

THE USES AND ABUSES
OF SECRET INTELLIGENCE

*Here Senator Church attacks and William Colby defends
the Central Intelligence Agency and its record. In what
must be one of the most remarkable understatements of
the epoch, the Senator declares that "the CIA has performed unevenly." It is imperative, he says, for us to have
a strong and effective intelligence service. What concerns
him are "the dark arts of secret intervention in foreign
countries"—the "covert operations" at the service of
"reactionary and repressive regimes that can never, for
long, escape or withstand the volcanic forces of change."
He places the blame primarily on our obsession with communism and the "illusion of American omnipotence."
Even so, Senator Church does not call for prohibition of
all clandestine activities, but they must be "consistent
either with the imperative of national survival" or with
our traditional belief in free governments. Later, in the
discussion that follows, the Senator indicates he thinks
the remedy is stricter legal guidelines and better congressional oversight.*

*Mr. Colby speaks about "what intelligence does for
peace." The "old intelligence," he concedes, "made some
mistakes and did some misdeeds" and conflicted "with
our ideal of openness," but "the new intelligence itself
rooted out and corrected" such errors. Nevertheless, Mr.
Colby says it is still necessary "to employ the older techniques of secret intelligence" against "societies and*

political systems that cling tenaciously to secrecy as a basis for power" and thus "can threaten our peace." The new intelligence, as Mr. Colby sees it, will achieve "a new concept of responsibility" through better guidelines which guard against infringement of rights of Americans, better suprvision by the Executive, Congress and even the Judiciary, and "better protection for those secrets we need to keep." It is, he concludes, "vitally important to America that our citizens regain their respect and trust in our intelligence service" because it is "essential for keeping America strong, free and at peace."

CIA and Obsessions
of the Cold War

Frank Church

Two hundred years ago, at the founding of this nation, Thomas Paine observed that "Not a place upon earth might be so happy as America. Her situation is remote from all the wrangling world. . . ." I still believe America remains the best place on earth, but it has long since ceased to be "remote from all the wrangling world."

On the contrary, even our internal economy now depends on events far beyond our shores. The energy crisis, which exposed our vulnerable dependence upon foreign oil, made the point vividly.

It is also tragic but true that our own people can no longer be made safe from savage destruction hurled down upon them from the most hidden and remote regions on earth. Soviet submarines silently traverse the ocean floors carrying transcontinental missiles with the capacity to strike at our heartland. The nuclear arms race threatens to continue its deadly spiral toward Armageddon.

In this dangerous setting, it is imperative for the United States to maintain a strong and effective intelli-

Frank Church is a U.S. Senator from Idaho, Chairman of the Senate Select Committee on Intelligence and member of the Committee on Foreign Relations.

gence service. On this proposition we can ill afford to be of two minds. We have no choice other than to gather, analyze, and assess—to the best of our abilities—vital information on the intent and prowess of foreign adversaries, present or potential.

Without an adequate intelligence-gathering apparatus, we would be unable to gauge with confidence our defense requirements; unable to conduct an informed foreign policy; unable to control, through satellite surveillance, a runaway nuclear arms race. "The winds and waves are always on the side of the ablest navigators," wrote Gibbon. Those nations without a skillful intelligence service must navigate beneath a clouded sky.

With this truth in mind, the United States established by the National Security Act of 1947 a Central Intelligence Agency to collect and evaluate intelligence, and provide for its proper dissemination within the government. The CIA was to be a clearing house for other American intelligence agencies, including those of the State Department and the various military services. It was to be an independent, civilian intelligence agency whose duty it was, in the words of Allen Dulles, CIA Director from 1953-1961:

> To weigh facts, and to draw conclusions from those facts, without having either the facts or the conclusions warped by the inevitable and even proper prejudices of the men whose duty it is to determine policy and who, having once determined a policy, are too likely to be blind to any facts which might tend to prove the policy to be faulty.

"The Central Intelligence Agency," concluded Dulles, "should have nothing to do with policy." In this way, neither the President nor the Congress would be left with any of the frequently self-interested intelligence assessments afforded by the Pentagon and the State Department, to rely upon.

In its efforts to get at the hard facts, the CIA has performed unevenly. It has had its successes and its failures. The CIA has detected the important new Soviet weapons systems early on; but it has often over-estimated the growth of the Russian ICBM forces. The CIA has successfully monitored Soviet adherence to arms conttcontrol agreements, and given us the confidence to take steps toward further limitations; but it has been unable to predict the imminence of several international conflicts, such as the 1973 Arab-Israeli war. In a word, though it deserves passing marks for its intelligence work, the CIA has certainly not been infallible.

While one may debate the quality of the agency's performance, there has never been any question about propriety and necessity of its evolvement in the process of gathering and evaluating foreign intelligence. Nor have serious questions been raised about the means used to acquire such information, whether from overt sources, technical devices, or by clandestine methods.

What has become controversial is quite unrelated to intelligence, but has to do instead with the so-called covert operations of the CIA, those secret efforts to manipulate events within foreign countries in ways presumed to serve the interests of the United States. Nowhere are such activities vouchsafed in the statutory language which created the Agency in 1947. "No indication was given in the statute that the CIA would become a vehicle for foreign political action or clandestine political warfare," notes Harry Howe Ransom, a scholar who has written widely and thought deeply about the problems of intelligence in modern society. Mr. Ransom concludes that "probably no other organization of the federal government has taken such liberties in interpreting its legally assigned functions as has the CIA."

The legal basis for this political action arm of the CIA is very much open to question. Certainly the legislative history of the 1947 Act fails to indicate that Congress anticipated the CIA would ever engage in covert political warfare abroad.

The CIA points to a catch-all phrase contained in the 1497 Act as a rationalization for its operational prerogatives. A clause in the statute permits the Agency "to perform such other functions and duties related to intelligence affecting the national security as the National Security Council may, from time to time, direct." These vague and seemingly innocuous words have been seized upon as the green light for CIA intervention around the world.

Moreover, these interventions into the political affairs of foreign countries soon came to overshadow the Agency's original purpose of gathering and evaluating information. Just consider how far afield we strayed. For example:

— We deposed the government of Guatemala when its leftist leanings displeased us;

— We attempted to ignite a civil war against Sukarno in Indonesia;

— We intervened to restore the Shah to his throne in Iran, after Mossadegh broke the monopoly grip of British Petroleum over Iranian oil;

— We attempted to launch a counter-revolution in Cuba through the abortive landing of an army of exiles at the Bay of Pigs;

— We even conducted a secret war in Laos, paying Meo tribesmen and Thai mercenaries to do our fighting there.

All these engagements were initiated without the knowledge or consent of Congress.

No country was too small, no foreign leader too trifling, to escape our attention:

— We sent a deadly toxin to the Congo with the purpose of injecting Lumumba with a fatal disease;

— We armed local dissidents in the Dominican Republic, knowing their purpose to be the assassination of Trujillo;

— We participated in a military coup overturning the very government we were pledged to defend in South Vietnam; and when Premier Diem resisted, he and his brother were murdered by the very generals to whom we gave money and support;

— For years, we attempted to assassinate Fidel Castro and other Cuban leaders. The various plots spanned three administrations, and involved an extended collaboration between the CIA and the Mafia.

Whatever led the United States to such extremes? Assassination is nothing less than an act of war, and our targets were leaders of small, weak countries that could not possibly threaten the United States. Only once did Castro become an accessory to a threat, by permitting the Russians to install missiles on Cuban soil within range of the United States, and this was the one time when the CIA called off all attempts against his life.

The roots of these malignant plots grew out of the obsessions of the Cold War. When the CIA succeeded the Office of Strategic Services of World War II, Stalin replaced Hitler as the Devil Incarnate. Wartime methods were routinely adopted for peacetime use.

In those myopic years, the world was seen as up for grabs between the United States and the Soviet Union. Castro's Cuba raised the spectre of a Soviet outpost at America's doorstep. Events in the Dominican Republic appeared to offer an additional opportunity for the Russians and their allies. The Congo, freed from Belgian rule, occupied the strategic center of the African continent, and the prospect of Soviet penetration there was viewed as a threat to American interests in emerging Africa. There was a great concern that a communist takeover in Indochina would have a "domino effect" throughout Asia. Even the lawful election in 1970 of a Marxist president in Chile was still seen by some as the equivalent of Castro's conquest of Cuba.

In the words of a former Secretary of State, "A desperate struggle [was] going on in back alleys of world politics." Every upheaval, wherever it occurred, was likened to a pawn on a global chessboard, to be moved this way or that, by the two principal players. This led the

CIA to plunge into a full range of covert activities designed to counteract the competetive efforts of the KGB.

Thus, the United States came to adopt the methods and accept the value system of the "enemy." In the secret world of covert action, we threw off all restraints. Not content merely discreetly to subsidize foreign political parties, labor unions, and newspapers, the Central Intelligence Agency soon began to directly manipulate the internal politics of other countries. Spending many millions of dollars annually, the CIA filled its bag with dirty tricks—ranging from bribery and false propaganda to schemes to "alter the health" of unfriendly foreign leaders and undermine their regimes.

Nowhere is this imitation of KGB tactics better demonstrated than in the directives sent to CIA agents in the Congo in 1960. Instructions to kill the African leader Lumumba were sent via diplomatic pouch, along with rubber gloves, a mask, syringe, and a lethal biological material. The poison was to be injected into some substance that Lumumba would ingest, whether food or toothpaste. Before this plan was implemented, Lumumba was killed by Congolese rivals; but, nevertheless, our actions had fulfilled the prophesy of George Williams, an eminent theologian at the Harvard Divinity School, who once warned, "Be cautious when you choose your enemy, for you will grow more like him."

The imperial view from the White House reached its arrogant summit during the Administration of Richard Nixon. On September 15, 1970, following the election of Allende to be President of Chile, Richard Nixon summoned to the White House Henry Kissinger, Richard Helms, and John Mitchell. The topic was Chile. Allende, Nixon stated, was unacceptable to the President of the United States.

In his handwritten notes for this meeting, Nixon indicated that he was "not concerned" with the risks involved. As Director Helms recalled in testimony before the Senate Committee, "The President came down very hard that he wanted something done, and he didn't care how . . . . " To Helms, the order had been all-inclusive. "If I ever carried a marshal's baton in my knapsack out of the Oval Office," he recalled, "it was that day." Thus the President of the United States had given orders to the CIA to prevent the popularly-elected President of Chile from entering office.

To bar Allende from the Presidency, a military coup was organized, with the CIA playing a direct role in the planning. One of the major obstacles to the success of the mission was the strong opposition to a coup by the Commander-in-Chief of the Chilean Army, General Rene Schneider, who insisted that Chile's constitution be upheld. As a result of his stand, the removal of General Schneider became a necessary ingredient in the coup plans. Unable to get General Schneider to resign, conspirators in Chile decided to kidnap him. Machine guns and ammunition were passed by the CIA to a group of kidnappers on October 22, 1970. That same day General Schneider was mortally wounded on his way to work in an attempted kidnap, apparently by a group affiliated with the one provided weapons by the CIA.

The plot to kidnap General Schneider was but one of many efforts to subvert the Allende regime. The United States sought also to bring the Chilean economy under Allende to its knees. In a situation report to Dr. Kissinger, our Ambassador wrote:

> Not a nut or bolt will be allowed to reach Chile under Allende. Once Allende comes to power we shall do all within our power to condemn Chile and the Chileans to utmost deprivation and poverty, a policy designed for a long time to come to accelerate the hard features of a communist society in Chile.

The ultimate outcome, as you know, of these and other efforts to destroy the Allende government was a bloodbath which included the death of Allende and the installation, in his place, of a repressive military dictatorship.

Why Chile? What can possibly explain or justify such an intrusion upon the right of the Chilean people to self-determination? The country itself was no threat to us. It has been aptly characterized as a "dagger pointed straight at the heart of Antarctica."

Was it to protect American-owned big business? We now know that I.T.T. offered the CIA a million dollars to prevent the ratification of Allende's election by the Chilean Congress. Quite properly, this offer was rejected. But the CIA then spent much more on its own, in an effort to accomplish the same general objective.

Yet, if our purpose was to save the properties of large American corporations, that cause had already been lost. The nationalization of the mines was decided well before Allende's election; and the question of compensation was tempered by insurance against confiscatory losses issued to the companies by the United States government itself.

No, the only plausible explanation for our intervention in Chile is the persistence of the myth that communism is a single, hydra-headed serpent, and that it remains our duty to cut off each ugly head, wherever and however it may appear.

Ever since the end of World War II, we have justified our mindless meddling in the affairs of others on the ground that since the Russians do it, we must do it, too. The time is at hand to re-examine that thesis.

Before Chile, we insisted that communism had never been freely chosen by any people, but forced upon them against their will. The communists countered that they resorted to revolution because the United States would never permit the establishment of a communist regime by peaceful means.

In Chile, President Nixon confirmed the communist thesis. Like Caesar peering into the colonies from distant Rome, Nixon said the choice of government by the

Chileans was unacceptable to the President of the United States. The attitude in the White House seemed to be: If—in the wake of Vietnam—I can no longer send in the Marines, then I will send in the CIA.

But what have we gained by our policy of consummate intervention, compared to what we have lost?

— A "friendly" Iran and Indonesia, members of the OPEC cartel, which imposes extortionate prices on the Western World for indispensible oil?

— A hostile Laos that preferred the indigenous forces of communism to control imposed by Westerners, which smacked of the hated colonialism they had fought so long to overthrow?

— A fascist Chile, with thousands of political prisoners languishing in their jails, mocking the professed ideals of the United States throughout the hemisphere?

If we have gained little, what then have we lost? I suggest we have lost—or grievously impaired—the good name and reputation of the United States from which we once drew a unique capacity to exercise matchless moral leadership. Where once we were admired, now we are resented. Where once we were welcome, now we are tolerated, at best. In the eyes of millions of once friendly foreign people, the United States is today regarded with grave suspicion and distrust.

What else can account for the startling decline in American prestige? Certainly not the collapse of our military strength, for our firepower has grown immensely since the end of World War II.

Of course, our eagerness since then to enter Asian wars, at the very time Western colonialism was being driven out of the Orient, has cost us dearly. But, on the whole, we welcomed the emergence of the newly independent governments of the Third World and gave them aid in the most generous measure.

For the hundreds of billions we loaned or gave away in various forms of economic and military aid, the United States earned scant gratitude. Never has a government given so much to so many, with so little to show for it.

I must place the blame, in large measure, on the fantasy that it lay within our power to control other countries through the covert manipulation of their affairs. It formed part of a greater illusion that entrapped and enthralled our President—the illusion of American omnipotence.

Nevertheless, I do not draw the conclusion of those who now argue that all American covert operations must be banned in the future. I can conceive of a dire emergency when timely clandestine action on our part might avert a nuclear holocaust and save an entire civilization.

I can also conceive of circumstances, such as those existing in Portugal today, where our discreet help to democratic political parties might avert a forcible takeover by a communist minority, heavily subsidized by the Russians. In Portugal, such a bitterly-unwanted, Marxist regime is being resisted courageously by a people who earlier voted eighty-four percent against it.

But these are covert operations consistent either with the imperative of national survival or with our traditional belief in free government. If our hand were exposed helping a foreign people in their struggle to be free, we could scorn the cynical doctrine of "plausible denial," and say openly, "Yes, we were there—and proud of it."

We were there in Western Europe, helping to restore democratic governments in the aftermath of the Second World War. It was only after our faith gave way to fear that we began to act as a self-appointed sentinel of the status quo.

Then it was that all the dark arts of secret intervention—bribery, blackmail, abduction, assassination—were put to the service of reactionary and repressive regimes that can never, for long, escape or withstand the volcanic forces of change.

And the United States, as a result, became ever more identified with the claims of the old order, instead of the aspirations of the new.

The remedy is clear. American foreign policy, whether openly or secretly pursued, must be made to conform once more to our historic ideals, the same fundamental belief in freedom and popular government that once made us a beacon of hope for the downtrodden and oppressed throughout the world.

The New CIA—
What Intelligence
Does For Peace

William Colby

I would like to speak about what intelligence does for peace. The revelations of the recent past have probably led many to question what intelligence has to do with peace. Those revelations reflect things past, things that a new intelligence itself rooted out and corrected. We are now engaged in developing a new role for intelligence, one that reflects modern American precepts and values. We ask your cooperation and support in articulating this new role.

James R. Schlesinger once said that one of the primary social services expected from government is security. This can be gained, in the old Biblical phrase, by "a strong man armed in his camp." I think we have developed other ways to achieve security over the centuries, particularly in the past twenty-eight years during which American intelligence has matured and become the best in the world.

Intelligence now enables us to anticipate as well as to know. Anticipation allows us to arm ourselves, if such be

William Colby was Director of the Central Intelligence Agency at the time of the Pacem in Terris IV *Convocation.*

necessary, with the right weapon. We need not face the light and accurate slingshot with an unwieldly broadsword. Anticipation also allows us to deter aggressors, demonstrating by our protective shield the futility of attacking us.

But anticipation these days also presents us with an opportunity, beyond anything known in the past, to negotiate. When we have knowledge of a foreign weapons system in the research phase, we can then discuss a mutual agreement to forgo its development and deployment. This can save millions of dollars on both sides—which can then be spent on plowshares rather than on swords. Such, of course, was the result of our negotiations with the Soviet Union about antiballistic missile systems. Intelligence made a significant contribution to the negotiating process, but its ability to monitor actual compliance was crucial to concluding the agreement. Vast sums, estimated between 50 and 100 billion dollars, were saved because neither side had to build extensive ABM systems.

The anticipation made possible by good intelligence offers a greater contribution to peace than merely limiting weapons expenditures. Anticipating future disputes can permit their resolution while they are still only problems. Predicting crises and confrontations can permit conciliation and compromise before they occur. Suspicions and misunderstandings can be replaced by accurate perceptions that there are real problems on both sides. Men of good will can then work to resolve these problems through international conferences, through joint studies into the facts, or through recognition of mutual rights and interests.

I therefore believe it highly appropriate for intelligence to be invited to a discussion of how we obtain peace on earth. Intelligence has contributed to this end and will contribute even more in the future.

The problems of the future can result in conflict or cooperation. Consider:

— overpopulation and underproduction;

— nuclear proliferation;

— extremism and terrorism;

— the economic imbalances between rich and poor countries;

— the exploitation of hitherto inaccessible riches in the sea or in space;

— the interdependence of economies and even cultures;

— the acceleration of events by exponential improvements in transportation and communication.

We must have systematic knowledge of these complex subjects, full awareness of all our capabilities to deal with them, and an understanding of the intentions of the actors on the scene. Intelligence provides these. It is a tool to help America move toward peace with our fellow partners on this globe.

There are those, however, who contend that our intelligence has in the past and can in the future create the very problems that limit our hopes for peace. To them I say that their concept of intelligence is outmoded. When it looks at open societies, today's intelligence collects what is publicly available; uses technology to gather and process information that can be seen, heard, or sensed; and then carefully analyzes the bits and pieces of the jigsaw puzzles to provide an answer to the problems we face.

There are societies and political systems, however, that cling tenaciously to secrecy as a basis for power. Against these societies, which can threaten our peace, it is indeed necessary to employ the older techniques of secret intelligence developed for a world in which openness and free exchange were unobtainable. The thought processes and procedures that create such secret plans threaten our long-term hopes for peace among nations and peoples in the new open world we look toward.

We must avoid a repetition of our ingenuous belief in the 1920s that the world had been made safe for democracy and that gentlemen, in consequence, should not read other gentlemen's mail. If we can indeed achieve a world of gentlemen through the process of negotiation and resolution of the passions and ambitions of the past, then truly we can turn away also from the use of secret intelligence. But until that day, we hazard peace if we blind ourselves to realities, as the great democracies did during the 1930s.

The capability of intelligence quietly to influence foreign situations can—and has—contributed to peace. I do not contest that many of these operations in our history were more narrowly justified by their contribution to what was then seen as America's interest.

But in a number of instances, some quiet assistance to democratic and friendly elements enabled them to resist hostile and authoritarian groups in an internal competition over the future direction of their countries. Postwar Western Europe resisted communist political subversion, and Latin America rejected Cuban-stimulated insurgency. They thereby thwarted at the local level challenges that could have escalated to the international level.

That there can be debate as to the wisdom of any individual activity of this nature is agreed. That such a potential must be available for use in situations truly important to our country and the cause of peace is equally obvious.

Many of our citizens would express agreement with what I have said but still express concern that there is an inherent contradiction between the need of intelligence for secrecy and our constitutional structure of openness. They reject a hypocrisy that allows intelligence to operate while professing that it does not.

It is true that the old concept of intelligence did conflict with our ideal of openness. This contradiction was dealt with by a cautious averting of responsible supervision from what were viewed as the necessary unpleasantries of the world of intelligence. The members of Congress who said they did not want to know of our activities, the careful circumlocutions used in the directives developed for intelligence—these reflected a consensus that while intelligence was needed to protect America, America was unwilling to admit its use of intelligence.

As a result, intelligence made some mistakes and did some misdeeds. That these were truly few and far between over the years of its history is a credit to the patriotism and integrity of the men and women of intelligence, rather than to controls upon them. But that they did occur forced attention to the need to articulate the proper role of intelligence in America.

After Vietnam and Watergate, exposures of improper intelligence activities aroused concern and launched the current exhaustive investigations. Intelligence has cooperated with these reviews because we in intelligence believe the future of intelligence is important to our country. We also believe that intelligence must find its fully understood and accepted position in our constitutional structure.

We Americans recognize the need for secrets when our institutions cannot operate without them: witness our ballot box, our grand jury proceedings, and our protection of commercial secrets. Intelligence needs secrets or its agents are exposed; patriotic Americans contributing to their country are pilloried as fronts; and chinks in an adversary's armor are rapidly closed when we obligingly make them public.

We—all of us—must develop out of our current investigations a new concept of *responsible* American intelligence. It will be a further innovation that America can bring to the intelligence profession. We will do it in essentially three steps.

—We will articulate better guidelines for intelligence, spelling out what it properly can do and what it will not do. We will ensure that it is focused on foreign intelligence, and does not infringe the rights of our citizens.

—We will develop better supervision of intelligence by the Executive, by the Congress, and even, where necessary, by the Judiciary. Better external supervision of intelligence will certainly generate intensive internal supervision, ensuring that American intelligence complies with America's constitutional concepts.

—And we will develop better secrecy of those aspects of intelligence that really need it, while at the same time ending the old tradition of total secrecy of everything about intelligence. The stream, even flood, of intelligence secrets that have been exposed this year has brought home to every American the fact that we must have better protection for those secrets we need to keep.

The hostile groups exposing our intelligence personnel, the hasty headlining of important technical intelligence projects, or the arrogance of those revealing our country's proper and important secrets in the cause of a self-proclaimed "higher morality"—all these have demonstrated the weakness of our current procedures for protecting our necessary secrets. We need no Official Secrets Act muzzling our press or frightening our citizens, and we in intelligence do not ask for one. We do need to be able to discipline those who freely assume the obligation of secrecy as members of our profession and then willfully repudiate it. We are sure that we can obtain the same recognition of our intelligence profession's need for confidentiality that we extend to our doctors, our lawyers, and our journalists.

Taking these three essential steps will not be easy. But I believe that we are now turning to a debate of the real issues that face American intelligence rather than agonizing over the missteps of the past. It is my sincere hope that this debate will lead to the kind of changes that I have outlined for American intelligence. It is vitally important to America that our citizens regain their respect and trust in our intelligence service. There must be a national consensus that American intelligence serves America and honors the Constitution. There must be a consensus that American intelligence is properly guided, properly supervised, and capable of protecting its own secrets so it can protect America.

I believe that a strong and free America is essential if we are to move toward peace on earth. I believe that a truly American intelligence service is equally essential to keep America strong, free, and at peace.

II

SHOULD WE PROHIBIT
COVERT CIA OPERATIONS?

The presentations of Senator Church and Mr. Colby
raise a storm of debate among the commentators on the
panel, in which the principals join. The focus of the at-
tack is on covert operations. There is general agreement
among the panelists that intelligence gathering is a
necessary function, but all except Ray Cline feel strongly
that covert operations should be prohibited. This position
is taken strongly by Morton Halperin and—with a good
deal of emotion—by Charles Morgan. Covert operations,
Mr. Morgan points out, require cover stories and cover
stories require lying. And when top officials from the
President down lie, he says, this does serious damage to
the democratic process. Dr. Cline also objects to some
covert operations but feels that when they are in defense of
democracy and freedom they are both justified and
necessary. He is concerned that "the year-long bath of
James Bondish criticism . . . has nearly destroyed the ef-
fectiveness of our intelligence agencies in collecting in-
formation abroad." Congressman Andrew Young doubts
that the intelligence community and those responsible for
it have really profited from their errors. It is, he warns,
"almost a foregone conclusion that many of the mistakes
of the past will be repeated in the future." Senator Clai-
borne Pell, wondering whether covert operations should
be separated from intelligence collection, says "the more
fundamental question [is] if and when this nation should

be engaged in covert operations at all." Senator Church and Mr. Colby respond to some of these comments and politely cross swords over what CIA did and did not do in Chile.

Claiborne Pell:

The congressional investigations of the intelligence activities of the U.S. conducted under the direction of Senator Church and Congressman Pike have opened up an entirely new area of congressional oversight and participation in the foreign policy process of this government. That this is a long overdue activity of the Congress has been clearly brought out by the findings to date of the two congressional intelligence committees.

The problem that we now face and which I hope our panelists will address is, what should be done in light of what has been revealed about the operations of the CIA and its relationships with our agencies of the national security community?

I would like to illustrate the dilemma involved here by recounting a personal experience of my own. Late in 1960, after I was elected to the Senate but before I was actually sworn in, I visited Cuba. In fact, I was the last member of Congress to do so before I returned to Cuba in September, 1974. During the course of my visit I was struck by the fact that most of the Cubans who opposed the Castro regime were either dead, in prison, or had fled the coun-

---

Claiborne Pell is a U.S. Senator from Rhode Island and a member of the Committee on Foreign Relations.

try. Accordingly, I concluded that it would be a monumental mistake if the United States were to mount or support any kind of revolution in Cuba, since the only way such an effort could succeed was if the majority of the people were sympathetic to the idea.

I knew nothing of the Bay of Pigs planning that was going on at the time, but I did press my views strongly with the CIA. Ironic as it may seem, I presented my views to Allen Dulles and other senior members of his staff on the very day, I later learned, that the Bay of Pigs was chosen as the site of the ill-fated invasion. I got a polite hearing, but not a glimmer of the fateful planning was conveyed to me.

When I recounted all this to President Kennedy after the Bay of Pigs invasion failed, he admonished me for not having presented my views directly to him. This experience, which I am sure has been repeated many times, raises the very serious question of whether intelligence collection and evaluation should be separated from covert operations. There is also the more fundamental question of whether this nation should be engaged in covert operations at all.

Another issue which comes to mind which must be addressed is the accountability of the CIA for its activities, decisions and judgments. Here the Congress obviously must play a role, but what is the proper role or the proper scope of such an oversight? And how can there be a responsible discharge of that duty?

Finally, I would like to ask whether perhaps the congressional investigations have now served their purpose. Much of the publicity which has been given to the Senate and House investigations, which, I hasten to add, are entirely proper and long overdue, has tended to give the impression that the initials CIA stand for Conspiracy, Intrigue and Assassination.

My question is, where is the proper balance between the need to investigate and correct excesses by a few CIA officers and the need to restore the cooperation of foreign governments and contacts and the morals of our CIA people abroad?

Andrew Young:

This really has been an interesting introduction to the whole question of intelligence. The thing that disturbs me is that we talk about it all as though these were missteps of the past, as if we don't intend to or could ever do these things again. I would contend that our proclivity to deal with people who are clients and puppets rather than with people who are friends and brothers inevitably makes it almost a foregone conclusion that many of the mistakes of the past will be repeated in the future.

A distinction between intelligence-gathering and covert activities is probably too simple. Senator Church quoted a statement from Allen Dulles that the function of intelligence was to weigh the facts and to draw the conclusions from those facts, without having either warped by the inevitable and even proper prejudices of men whose duty it is to determine policy. I think that is almost an impossibility. And I would use as an illustration the present situation in Angola, where there is a war going on right now in which we are involved. Just how we're involved has never come before the Congress of the United States and yet all over Africa it is known and assumed and even admitted by a reporter from the *Washington Post* that there is very definitely an American para-military presence in Zaire supporting the FNLA.

All this is in spite of the fact that our support of Mubutu, the brother-in-law of the leader of the FNLA, clearly puts us on one side, the side that really doesn't make much sense in Africa because it is also the side of South Africa. All this, while right next door in Zambia there is a man of integrity, of neutrality, of enormous prestige, the son of a Presbyterian minister—Kenneth

Andrew Young is a member of the U.S. House of Representatives and a member of the House Rules Committee.

Kaunda—who sounds like one of our Founding Fathers in his statements about the founding of his country, Zambia.

It seems to me that our proper role, given what I understand about our appreciation of the democratic process and our determination for people to have the right to make their own decisions and determine their own destiny, should have been to back the neutralists in Angola and support the position of men like Kenneth Kaunda of Zambia and Julius Nyerere of Tanzania. They have been saying that all foreign influences should be withdrawn from Angola and that those African leaders in neighboring states, most of whom supported the liberation movements, should be supported in pulling together a coalition government.

For some reason, we didn't take that option. We, instead, chose sides. And choosing sides has put us not only in league with South Africa, but also involves some of the same moral complications that the Soviet Union is confronted with in supplying massive weapons for blacks to kill blacks, and extending the Cold War into Southern Africa.

When this kind of mistake goes on after Vietnam and in the presence of the kind of debate that's taking place in both the House and the Senate, it says to me we have not yet learned what a truly American intelligence operation is.

I would say a truly American intelligence is an intelligence that respects the emergent leadership and that somehow finds a way to support openly the values of change in a democratic process. Somehow covert and clandestine activities to preserve civilization are to me a contradiction in terms. For any civilization not built on trust and freedom is hardly worth the term civilization.

I agree that we do have to have an information-gathering agency and that information about the rest of the world, intelligence in fact, is necessary to survive in this kind of world. But I think the decision-making process in a secret agency which tends to create gaps in accountability, because those at the top don't really want to know how the job gets done at the bottom, produces values different from the values of a truly American intelligence operation.

Morton Halperin:

The two interesting main presentations reveal where the current debate stands. Senator Church gave us an outline of the horrors that have been performed in our name— those which Mr. Colby has chosen to call the "small mistakes," few and far between, in covert operations in a variety of countries in the world, using means contrary to our ideals—assassination, kidnapping, fake documents and so on. These activities have mainly been based upon objectives which were contrary to what we stand for, such actions as subverting the democratic processes of Chile and interfering in the internal affairs of Cuba and of the Congo and of other countries.

Mr. Colby has told us that this is the Old Intelligence, that the Old Intelligence has passed from the scene, that it has reformed itself and that we now have something called the New Intelligence, which merely works for peace and no longer does these other things. And Senator Church has told us that we should put our faith back in our democratic institutions and that the solution to the problem is that somehow we should bring the activities of our intelligence agencies under democratic control and have them pursue our democratic ideals.

As far as intelligence-gathering goes, it seems to me we have no choice but to try. It is clearly the case that we need intelligence about certain activities, although one suspects that the appetite of the intelligence community for information, not only about Americans but about foreigners also, extends far beyond that of our political

Morton Halperin is the Director of the Project for National Security and Civil Liberties at the Center for National Security Studies of the Fund for Peace; and former Deputy Assistant Secretary of Defense.

leadership. Nevertheless, it is clear that we need some information about potential adversaries and about potential dangers in the world. And, therefore, we need some kind of intelligence-gathering ability. I would argue that it is vitally important that we take the kind of steps that Mr. Colby suggests to bring that capability under control. This means that we need legislation by Congress saying precisely what the intelligence agencies can and cannot do in terms of gathering intelligence.

Further, we need to back up such legislation with effective laws which make it a crime for intelligence agencies to violate their charter, so that Mr. Colby's predecessor as Director of the CIA does not send a memo to the President's Assistant for National Security Affairs saying to treat the attached document carefully because it violates our charter to write it, and then they both file the document away and go about their business. It must be made a crime, I would argue, for the intelligence organizations to violate their charters. And legislation has to be backed up by effective public controls and effective congressional controls.

I think it is an absolute delusion to believe that we can bring covert operations under democratic controls and have them conform to our democratic ideals. It is my view that, in fact, covert operations are simply inconsistent with the American constitutional system, inconsistent with the notion that we stand for democratic ideals in the world, and that the time has come for the United States to abolish its covert operations and to make them illegal.

Both Senator Church and Mr. Colby said that that cannot be done. They both created before us a horrible hypothetical situation in which the future is said to depend on preventing some group from seizing a nuclear weapon somewhere, or some other horrible hypothetical situation which requires us to maintain capabilities for covert operations. In my view, such situations are extraordinarily unlikely. And it is even more unlikely that a covert capability such as we have maintained would be effective.

Senator Church in his Committee report already dealt with hypothetical problems in relation to assassinations and suggested that the Constitution is not a suicide pact. Senator Church in his report also indicated that the President always has the right to take action in truly extreme situations where the survival of the United States depends upon it, and then to come before the Congress and the public and ask for approval or disapproval.

The problem with maintaining a capability for covert operations, however, and the problem with letting our Presidents conduct such operations is that they will tell us that they will only do this in grave extremes, when the survival of the nation truly depends upon it. But, in fact, as long as we have that capability and as long as our Presidents have the authority to use it, they will use it in non-extreme situations. They will use it in situations when the security of the United States does not depend on it, and they will use it in situations where they know that they cannot get the public and the congressional support which would enable them to proceed to other means to effect the will of the United States.

It seems to me that the assertion that we no longer have any operations in free and open societies, as Mr. Colby has suggested here, must depend on a very strained definition of an open society. Because it is now clear that we have operations in Portugal, it is now clear that we have operations in Angola. It is beyond question that we have operations in the Azores. I would not define any of these as closed societies, as Mr. Colby seemed to by using the term. I think it is a fact that as long as these capabilities exist, they will be used in a variety of different places, in places where the executive branch believes, as it did in the past, that our national security is involved and where it is not prepared to subject that decision and that policy to open and public debate.

It is no accident that we resort to the method of

covert operations when what we are doing conflicts with our ideals, when what we are doing is something that could not get the support of the Congress or the public in the United States. In my view there is no way to bring that process under democratic control. There is no way to give the President final authority and expect him to use it only in dire emergencies or only in support of American ideals. As long as that capability exists it will be used to subvert the constitutional processes of decision-making at home and to subvert our ideals abroad.

So I would suggest that if we honestly look at the kind of abuses of the covert operations process that Senator Church's Committee has brought out we will conclude the only effective step we can take, and one not at all inconsistent with our own survival, is to abolish covert operations.

Ray S. Cline:

I noted that Senator Church kindly said that he didn't expect complete infallibility from the CIA and then rather reproachfully said that he had found some of their work fallible. I thought infallibility was reserved for another institution. Naturally, I'm speaking of the one on Capitol Hill.

I find myself always at a disadvantage in following such eloquent speakers and people of high moral certitude as the Senator and my friend Morton Halperin. I would like to speak much more personally and informally, if I may, and very bluntly. Like Bill Colby I spent thirty years in intelligence work in the State Department and in the CIA. My last duty in the CIA was in 1966, so I feel I'm a little bit impartial on what's been happening to the agency lately. If you have had to meet a secret intelligence payroll

Ray S. Cline is the Executive Director of Studies at the Georgetown Center for Strategic and International Studies; former Director of Intelligence and Research, Department of State; former Director of Intelligence, Central Intelligence Agency.

you sometimes have a more disturbing view of the problems of our intelligence agencies.

In the twenty-eight years of intelligence activity, as Mr. Colby says, the central intelligence system, which includes the State Department and the Defense agencies as well as the CIA, has conducted, I suppose, millions of operations, millions of activities. I believe that in the fifties and sixties, CIA and the other agencies constituted the best peacetime central intelligence system in the world. It included scholars. I was deputy director of the analytical and reporting element, which had to select items daily for the President, had to write national intelligence estimates, and had to try to see that the collection of intelligence around the world met the requirements of our decision-making process. That's what intelligence is really all about.

I'm happy to see that every speaker so far, with the possible exception of Mr. Halperin, agrees that those functions are worthwhile. I've had the feeling sometimes that Mr. Halperin is so worried about covert operations that he would abolish the whole structure of government if it was necessary to prevent them.

I admit freely, as Mr. Colby does, that in those twenty-eight years some very serious mistakes were made. Some of them were in the gray areas where responsibilities and guidelines were inadequate for what, after all, was a new profession, a new part of government, in our system. Misinterpretations were quite possible, and some were made. The worst indiscretions, however, in my view, were in following direct orders from Presidents of the United States to become involved in internal security functions properly the task of other agencies of government.

I suppose that we would all like, in hindsight, to think that we would flatly say "No" to the President if he ordered a questionable activity. I've always found heroism a great deal more palatable after the fact than in the crucial moment. I would like to suggest that what we need to do, particularly in view of the agreement here about the importance of the main functions of intelligence—leaving covert actions aside for the moment—is to adopt some legislative and administrative remedies and a monitoring mechanism which would prevent the excesses or aberrations which have been noted. I would like to get the executive branch of this government, and the congressional branch, to move ahead to recreate the kind of intelligence system we so badly need.

My fear and my own conviction is that the year-long bath of James Bondish criticism of the intelligence agencies, particularly CIA, has nearly destroyed the effectiveness of our intelligence agencies in collecting information abroad. It has discredited and demoralized the people in the intelligence system, many of whom have never done anything but read newspapers, read foreign intelligence reports, write scholarly essays and report to the Congress, to the White House, to the State Department and to the Defense Department.

Furthermore, all this has given the impression abroad that the CIA is a criminal institution with which it is unpalatable to deal. I can assure you we cannot operate effectively in the international arena if we have destroyed our own institutions. I would like to suggest that the Congress establish what I felt the need for for so many years and what the Congress never established, a Joint Congressional Committee of Oversight, one which has the real leadership of the House and the Senate represented in it. Such a Joint Committee should concentrate on a national intelligence policy and the kind of programs that we need, not on single copy poison dart guns or shellfish poison which is never used, but on the kind of system we need and the kind of activities we need.

I think we should also have clearly established in new legislation more precise than the 1947 Act that the intelligence community is a permanent peacetime part of the political process, of decision-making in this country, with whatever guidelines and monitoring provisions are deemed necessary, and that there will be an analytical service preparing reports of various levels of secrecy for the White House, for the National Security Council and for the Congress.

I believe it would be feasible for a great deal of this to be done for the public so that our communities of scholars could be brought into the process of understanding the very complicated and dangerous world which exists around us. Naturally, the collection systems which are our eyes and ears should be developed progressively and imaginatively as they were over the past twenty years because they provide the hardware data, the gross information on which our security rests. But I also want to remind you that you cannot take a picture or overhear what is going on silently in somebody's mind.

I agree with Mr. Colby that we need the best kind of human source intelligence collection in the world. We are in a very exposed position, and there is no great nation which is not running a lot of intelligence collection operations against us with human beings as well as technical sources.

Finally, let me say just a word about the nasty subject of covert political action. Most people discuss it as if it were a social disease. I think the fact that every successive President of this country has felt, in the interests of security, that some kind of covert political action was necessary ought to make us at least consider what the purposes are. Some of those purposes were misguided, and I make no brief for the Bay of Pigs operation, for example. I also feel that the secret Laos army to which Senator Church referred, when it became too large and paramilitary and almost overt, was not an appropriate clandestine function. On the other hand, I regret very much the fact that a very small minority of the Laotian people have just deposed a centuries-old monarchy which was presiding over the fate of the most peaceful people in Southeast Asia until the North Vietnamese came in and organized a tightly disciplined para-military force.

I believe there are places in the world where the

United States has a responsibility for resisting the establishment of one-party dictatorships, totalitarian societies and para-military operations when the people in those countries want to resist them and want our help.

Senator Church spoke, properly, of the great achievements of this country in stabilizing Western Europe in the devastating aftermath of World War II. The Marshall Plan was a distinguished economic achievement. The NATO alliance put a security military cordon around the area. But I can assure you that if the Central Intelligence Agency had not been supporting organs of freedom of information and parliamentary political parties in Italy and France and West Germany, the face of Western Europe today would be quite different because of the strenuous efforts being made by Stalinist Russia to create one-party dictatorships in those old democracies. I do not feel we should ever legislate ourselves out of the possibility of coming to the defense of like-minded people around the world, quietly and secretly, with political assistance, which usually means simply giving advice and money to people who are seeing their opponents armed and financed from outside the country in the interests of the non-democratic societies.

May I conclude by saying that I read the 344-page report issued by the Church Committee with great interest. I am a little nonplussed by the fact that one of the conclusions is that nobody got assassinated. I hope that in subsequent reports the Senator will give equal time to the achievements of the CIA and the hopes for a good intelligence operation. For we have exposed much of the processes of government and have named a lot of names in order to demonstrate that a serious thought was being given to the assassination of Fidel Castro by Cubans at the time when our government's policy was to send ashore a 1,400-manned, armed force of Cubans to try to destroy Castro's whole regime. I'm not sure that was a wise policy, but it does not surprise me that the government included in it the possibility of arming small infiltration bands as well as large para-military forces.

What does seem clear to me is that Fidel Castro is alive and well in Havana and that we need a good intelligence system to go on with other parts of the business. I am also a little distressed that Fidel Castro is sending thousands of armed guerillas, organized by the KGB, the Soviet intelligence service which dominates the Cuban intelligence service, to assist in communist revolutions in Portugal, in Angola, and I'm sure in the Middle East.

I do not see that we can take comfort in the kind of activity which is going on in the world at large. In my view, for us to take every measure possible to support our kinds of institutions abroad is very important for this country. The CIA has a very small role to play in that kind of action, but I think it would be very wrong of our Congress to make it impossible for future Presidents to play that role when it is appropriate and when it would be effective.

Charles Morgan:

The function of the CIA, I believe, is the function of the Pinkertons, international company cops. And our vital national interests involve a thousand military posts around the world and the protection of American corporate interests. Senator Church, the reason we overthrew Mr. Allende, a democratically elected leader, is purely and simply because we had economic interests there. It is the same reason, I suppose, that we didn't put in jail the man who offered a million dollar bribe to a federal agency to overthrow a democratically elected leader.

The problem is not what we're discussing here; the problem is that we have an army that can't win a war in the world and a concept called democracy that we don't

Charles Morgan was Washington Executive Director of the American Civil Liberties Union (A.C.L.U.) at the time of the Pacem in Terris IV *convocation.*

believe in because we can't practice it at home. It involves a phrase that George Wallace—of all people—is utilizing in his campaign for President. Imagine what the slogan of Wallace is: "Trust the People." There's nothing wrong with that except that we don't practice it.

Our ethics have changed. The entire population of the United States knows that the government lies. In a democracy, that becomes a civil liberties issue because the people are entitled to be confronted with facts upon which to vote. That's the essence of what Jefferson meant when he talked about education.

Covert activities require cover stories and cover stories are a euphemism for lying. It is implicit and inherent in the beast.

Church:

Of course, Mr. Morgan is right when he says that covert action, particularly of the kinds that I find so objectionable, require cover stories and thus force Presidents from time to time into a position of lying. And then there's this doctrine of plausible denial that has grown up within the intelligence community. You want to design the covert action in such a way that when the facts do surface—which in time they always do—then it will be possible for the President, as the spokesman of our government, plausibly to deny our connection with the operation. That's where we get into such serious trouble.

The point of my original remarks really had to do with confirming covert operations either to the imperatives of national survival, the avoidance of nuclear wars, or something of that grave character. Or conforming them to the historic principles of our nation. Then if the facts do surface we won't have to lie about it. We can say, yes, we helped the people of Portugal, if those were the facts. Eighty-five percent of them want a democracy. And the Russians were pushing all kinds of money in to impose a communist regime with a military government, and we tried to help democratic parties stay alive and we're proud of it. We don't have to lie about that, because it conforms to our own principles and values.

Mr. Cline complains that our Committee's efforts to find the truth have demoralized and all but destroyed the Central Intelligence Agency. Well, it depends on your point of view. I got up one morning the other day and there were two articles by two distinguished columnists commenting on the work of the Committee. One of them took Mr. Cline's line and said because the Committee had struck down on the Agency with a mailed fist the Agency was in shambles, all but utterly dismantled and destroyed. And the other distinguished columnist said that the Committee had dealt with the Agency with such a velvet glove that it had all but abandoned its duty to conduct an honest investigation. I figured that morning that we might be doing it right.

One should remember this investigation commenced because of charges of the most serious and unlawful wrongdoings, directed inward on the American people in some cases and directed outward against foreign people, including certain foreign leaders, in other cases. These charges surfaced in the free press, and once they surfaced they had to be investigated. It was not this Committee and not the Congress that has caused whatever trouble exists in these agencies. It was these activities that were wrong. And when they began to surface they had to be investigated. The only way you're going to get them right is to get the facts out and make the reforms that are necessary to correct them.

As far as moral certitude is concerned, I think all of us know enough about it to understand the difference between a Portugal and a Chile, and to understand the difference between the Greek colonels and the efforts to restore democratic government in Western Europe after the war.

With respect to Mr. Halperin's remarks, I have just this comment to make. I understand and I have struggled with the dilemma that Mr. Halperin points out, the dilemma that, if you have the apparatus, how can you be sure that it will conform to standards that the American people would approve? How can we be certain that Presidents will not abuse such power if it is within their reach and if they think they can get by with it? How can you harness the beast?

Mr. Halperin says you can't, and therefore you must make all covert operations illegal. I have enough faith in our system to think we can. It means that we must write definite restrictions into the law with respect to covert operations in the future. We've started out with a report on assassinations in which we recommend adding to the criminal code of this country appropriate provisions against conspiracies or attempts to assassinate foreign leaders. And there must be other restrictions written into the law on covert operations. We mustn't leave it just to the President to decide. The Congress has its responsibility, too, and I think an appropriate Joint Committee of the Congress, currently informed and consulted in connection with all covert activities, would be the watchdog that, in conjunction with the appropriate restrictions in the law, could keep covert operations within proper bounds. I think it is worth a try.

Colby:

I'm delighted to see that almost all the participants here seem to believe in intelligence and even secret intelligence, except for my old colleague, Mr. Morgan. I was once a member of the A.C.L.U. and helped represent it in a case. He seems to say that we ought to fire "that spy in the Kremlin." I don't want to fire that spy in the Kremlin. He's a pretty valuable fellow. I really think that would be a mistake. But the rest of us seem to agree on the necessity for intelligence and even secret intelligence. So I think we should pass on to the more debatable questions, especially the question of proper covert action.

Covert action, of course, can be conducted under our statutes. It is also something that has been undertaken by Presidents throughout our history, for many, many years. In fact, Benjamin Franklin was associated with a covert action program in France designed to move weapons to some embattled colonists out in America without committing France to active participation in the effort. I think that would be considered by most of us as the right frame of reference for covert action. I just point out that we apparently have been doing this for years.

We have also undertaken some rather silly covert actions. President Grant sent some people up to Canada to try to entice certain of the provinces to defect from Canada and join the United States. That was a rather conspicuous failure, but he thought that he had the Constitutional authority to do it, and there wasn't much protest about it.

The Congress, of course, has already faced the question of whether the United States should engage in covert action. And the Congress knows that the United States does so. All of our Congressmen knew about the Bay of Pigs shortly after it happened. And there were a variety of other ways in which the Congress was kept advised of covert action. Last year, you will recall, both the House and the Senate posed the question of whether we should abolish covert action, and very specific bills were proffered. Both chambers said no by a three-to-one vote. I'll go with that vote. There are people who feel that we should cease to engage in covert action. But I think that most Americans feel that we must have this kind of weapon in our national arsenal for use whenever it is appropriate. But when is it appropriate and when isn't it?

"Plausible denial" was part of the mythology of covert action in earlier years. This concept held that the President could deny responsibility for an intelligence

operation and not be proven false. A contradiction arose,
however, when President Eisenhower was faced with the
fact that a U-2 was shot down in the Soviet Union. We put
out a cover story that it was a missing weather plane.
Mr. Krushchev pointed out in his memoirs that he was
going to have some fun with us on that.

President Eisenhower was faced with the dilemma
that if he asserted that the plane was a weather plane he
would be proven wrong, but if he said that he did not
know of its intelligence mission it would appear that he
was not running his own government. Even though Allen
Dulles offered to resign, it was quite obvious that the
President could not deny responsibility. That incident was
the death knell of the concept of "plausible denial." I've
pointed out to our own employees that it is not a viable
theory anymore because it contradicts our American Constitutional structure and that the responsibility goes up
to our senior leadership.

The question of lies and cover stories came up in my
confirmation hearing, among other places, and it came up
particularly in a story that quoted Allen Dulles as having
said that he would lie to anybody but the President.
Actually, if you look at what Mr. Dulles said in the tran-
script of the Warren Commission hearings, when he was
asked whether he would reveal a certain agent who
worked for him, he said: "Well, first, I wouldn't lie to the
President, I wouldn't conceal this from the President. To
other people I wouldn't say what was there."

There is a distinction between a lie and refusal to
comment about things that you don't want to comment
about, to keep them secret. The distinction that we can
make in America is to refuse to reveal certain things but
not to actively lie in the process. I have said, and I have
tried to stick to this, that I won't lie to the American people and I won't lie to the Congress. But I think that I do
have the right and even the duty to refuse to comment on
certain things.

As for covert actions, I recognize there are debates about the wisdom or lack of wisdom of various operations. However, as President Kennedy said, "our successes are unheralded and our failures are trumpeted." Quite a few of the successes come out later and are somehow put into a context which makes them appear to be failures. I think the war in Laos is an example.

I have always maintained that the war in Laos was a success. A number of countries were interested in Laos. The North Vietnamese were moving troops in there, trying to take it over. We made an agreement, between about fifteen nations in Geneva in 1962, that all of us would remove our forces and paramilitary people from Laos and that it would be neutral and independent. We removed all of our military and paramilitary people—about 1500. The North Vietnamese removed 40 of their 7,000. Then they began to push around the people in the Laotian hills, and President Kennedy was faced with a problem. Was he going to let this happen, or was he going to send in the Marines? He didn't want to send in the Marines or the Army or anybody else, nor did he want to just sit and watch it happen. So he asked the CIA if it could help. And the CIA did help for ten years. It committed a very large contingent of CIA people—by CIA standards—into that operation, some two or three hundred officers. He also spent a large amount of money—by CIA standards—on that operation, some tens of millions of dollars a year.

At the end of the ten years the battle lines were about where they were in 1963, although the North Vietnamese strength had increased from 7,000 to 70,000. I think that was a pretty good story, because at the end of the ten years we achieved a coalition government and a neutral and independent Laos and a reassertion by all the parties that they would respect the independence and neutrality of Laos. Since then, of course, the communist element of that particular coalition, with continued assistance from North Vietnam, threw out the other parties, while assistance from the United States terminated as a result of the agreement.

Laos is a long way away. One can debate whether aid to Laos is in our national interest at any time. But I think the CIA did the job the government asked it to do. It did it effectively, and it made a contribution to freedom in that distant part of the world.

As for the CIA's responsiveness to the American people on covert action, Congress did insist last year that any such covert action be revealed to Congress and that the CIA not even have the potential to conduct covert actions without the knowledge of Congress. The 1974 Act provided that any CIA activities other than intelligence-gathering required a presidential finding that such activities were important to the national security. It further provided that such activities be reported in a timely fashion to the appropriate committees of the Congress. There are six such appropriate committees.

The CIA is in full compliance with that Act with respect to any activity of the CIA anywhere in the world outside of pure intelligence-gathering. I think that Act provides a mechanism for the people's representatives in Congress to decide whether the kind of covert action we actually undertake at any one time is appropriate for our country, or is a mistake. This is a process which involves joint responsibility for decisions on these important issues.

I hope that these six committees will be reduced by some kind of consolidation. It not only takes time to report separately to each, but I have noticed a rather short period elapses from the moment when I brief all six committees to the moment when I read an article about that particular briefing on the front page of the newspapers. But I still think these necessary activities must be conducted in compliance with our Constitution and that this goal can be achieved through sharing responsibility between the Executive and the people's representatives in Congress.

Pell:

I would hope as we move along we could discuss the question of whether covert activities should be moved out from under the same roof as the intelligence-collection and assessment ones. My experience in Cuba left me with the very firm conclusion that there should be a separation here. Those who have a commitment to the covert operation will attempt to cut the cloth of these intelligence assessments to suit their purposes. I would like to see this discussed later on by the members of the panel. But now Dr. Cline has indicated that he would respond to the responders.

Cline:

I left this government in November, 1973, because I was dissatisfied with what we now call the Watergate Syndrome, and I feel my moral position to comment is at least as good as that of other citizens in this country. I think the reasonable conclusion from the fact that these representatives of the Congress of the United States and Director Colby of the Central Intelligence Agency are here at this table discussing these issues with remarkable candor is a refutation of the view that all of the institutions of the U.S. government are rotten and full of liars.

I would like to say just one other thing. I would like to feel that there has been from the serious discussion here a remarkable unity in views, that is, that intelligence collection and analysis and assessment is vital, and that there is a serious problem and a difficulty in managing covert operations. What I hope is that this group and the Congress, Senator Church's Committee and Congressman Pike's Committee, will work with the executive branch and, with full explanation to the people of the country, figure out what kind of an intelligence organization we want and what we want it to do.

The intelligence agencies in my view have never been out of control. They have been following instructions, sometimes mistakenly. Perhaps they should not have followed instructions. But if clear guidelines are presented, particularly if they are represented in legislation, I can assure you from thirty years of experience of working with people who felt they were patriotically motivated, that they will follow properly constituted instructions by the properly constituted authorities of the United States government.

Morgan:

I want to correct Mr. Cline's impression. I don't think that all the institutions of the American government are rotten. As a matter of fact I think we ought to try some of them more often. The Constitution of the United States provides for a declaration of war. If we declare war, then we should go to war, or we should aid other countries openly and aboveboard. If another country or a group in another country promotes democracy and wants democracy, if our national interests are democracy, then why can't we openly fund them, discuss them, talk about them? If we're proud of them we can do that.

Everyone in the United States government, of course, is not a liar. Some adopt, as Mr. Colby wisely does, the kind of approach where you just don't tell folks. That certainly beats lying. The Constitution provides for that in the Fifth Amendment. But the government of the United States and the salaries of government employees are still paid by the people in this country. And there is an obligation to acquaint the people with the facts about how their government is run, especially in peacetime. If we have gone so far in this country that we do not understand that, then we are over the hill.

Senator Pell, you seem to think the debate is whether we should have covert activities openly or not openly. My position is that we should abolish them altogether.

I believe I agree with Mr. Cline that the CIA does what it's supposed to do. They are not a rogue elephant off on an enterprise of their own, Senator, they're just plain folks going out and doing what in the hell they're told to do, whatever it is.

One thing more. You, Senator Pell, ask the question about covert activity in terms of whether we are going to have good ones or bad ones. This is not the question before the American people. The question before the American people is: why do they think their government lies?

Pell:

Maybe the answer is there should be no covert activity. But that is a decision for government to make and for the American people to make. If there are covert activities, however, then you have to find out where the balance is in the investigation to correct the excesses of the CIA and also you have to have some cooperation from foreign governments and contacts. This is what the purpose of this panel is all about. What is that balance? In my own view, we've just about reached it now, and this is probably the watershed time.

Halperin:

I would like to say a word about this question of whether the CIA is a rogue elephant off on its own, or, as Mr. Cline tells us, is always obeying the orders of the President. I think the latter would be absolutely remarkable—indeed, the CIA would be the only institution in the history of the world which always obeyed its orders and never lied to its superiors. On the other hand, I think the record suggests that the CIA is not an organization that has been going off in large measure ignoring the orders of its Presidents. Most of the things that the CIA has done and that the FBI has done are the things that our Presidents wanted them to do. And I think nobody can read the description of the Lumumba assassination in the report of Senator Church's Committee without thinking that President Eisenhower, if he didn't want to know that Lumumba was going to be assassinated, certainly wanted him out of the picture and didn't care at all how that was done. Nor is there any doubt in my mind that Lyndon Johnson wanted the CIA to find out as much about the antiwar movement in the U.S. as he could get it to do.

At the same time, I think one does have to say that we know of certain cases in which the agency, like all other agencies, deliberately disobeyed the President or failed to consult the President when it knew it was doing something wrong. And the difference between the CIA and other agencies is that when it does that it often can have very substantial consequences. For example, we know that the CIA opened thousands of letters of citizens going to and from many different countries for a twenty-year period, knowing that it was illegal and never getting around to telling the President of the United States that that program was going on. And the consequence of that was that many of us, including Richard Nixon, Senator Church and a great many other people, had their mail opened, copied and filed, without the orders of the President and in direct violation of the law. So one cannot say the CIA never knowingly violates the law.

It is also clear from the report of Senator Church's Committee that when Lyndon Johnson attempted to be sure that his government was not trying to assassinate Castro, and tried to find out whether we had previously tried to do so, he got a report from Richard Helms in which Helms failed to tell the President of the view of the Inspector General of the CIA that we were then conducting an operation which the Inspector General thought was an assassination attempt against Mr. Castro. The President was left with a view that even if it had gone on in the past it had then been stopped.

It also is clear that Mr. Helms did not tell Mr. McCone about that, because as he explained to the Committee, Mr. McCone was new in intelligence matters and might not quite understand what it was all about. And so it was better to let it go forward a little and then if we were on the point of pulling the trigger perhaps he would consult with Mr. McCone. So I think that it's not true that the CIA is totally out of control. But I think it is true that we cannot count on it always to obey the law or always to obey the directives of the President.

Church:

I want to compliment Mr. Halperin for his statement because it puts this whole thing in perspective. I'm a little sensitive about it because I was one who first made the statement about the rogue elephant. There is evidence in the report that bears out that from time to time there was that kind of behavior here. There's also evidence in the report that at other times the CIA was clearly conforming with presidential directives.

Somehow that rogue elephant remark struck a chord, or discord, because Barry Goldwater came up to me and he was quite furious about it. And I said, "Why, Barry? There is evidence that would lead one to suspect that at times the agency may have behaved like a rogue elephant." And he said, "I don't care anything about that, but the next time you refer to the Agency in those terms, please refer to it not as a rogue elephant but as a wild jackass."

Stewart R. Mott:

I gather from what Mr. Cline and Mr. Colby and Frank Church have said that they do find allowable areas for

---

Stewart Mott, who chaired this session, is a member of the Board of Trustees of The Fund for Peace and a member of the Board of Directors of the Center for the Study of Democratic Institutions.

covert action. But I wonder if, within the bounds of what the law should provide, we should allow the CIA or its operatives knowingly to break the criminal code of the United States or of any foreign country.

Colby:

In the United States, I would say certainly not. But most foreign countries have laws against espionage, and it would be very difficult indeed to conduct our intelligence operation without breaking a few of those.

Cline:

I think there is a misunderstanding about most covert action in believing that it is organizing armies and conducting vast illegal campaigns. In my view, the most successful covert intelligence operations are those in which no law is broken and in which the American point of view and in many cases financial assistance is given to constructive elements in foreign societies. So far as I know, that doesn't break any foreign law. It is like giving a campaign contribution to Senator Church, which I hope many of you are doing.

What I want to say is that I hope the Congress and the executive branch decide to do just what Senator Church said, that if we want to fight an undeclared war against Cuba or the Congo or Vietnam or wherever, we ought to have the guts to say it is a war and fight with all the means we have. I don't think we ought to give the job to the CIA in hopes that it can be done quietly and secretly and nobody will notice it.

Those kinds of activities, those kinds of covert actions, in fact, are the exceptions, the well-known cases which I hear every time I take part in such a discussion. The kind of covert action which I keep defining, such as that which assisted in stabilizing Western Europe, is not illegal, not immoral, and I think we ought to continue it.

Halperin:

Mr. Cline has suggested that what he hears is complaints about large covert operations. I don't think that's what we are complaining about here. Nor is it an answer to tell us that the great success was the support of democratic forces in Europe in 1948. When was the last time the CIA intervened on the side of liberal democratic forces in a country?

We keep being told about Europe in 1948. The kind of covert operation that I'm objecting to is the kind of covert operation that led the American government to go to the military of Chile and to the Christian Democratic Party of Chile and to say to them, "You may think that you're going to continue your constitutional processes and you may think that it's all right for your parliament to meet and lawfully elect Mr. Allende, but that is unacceptable to the United States and it stinks, and so if you go ahead with your democratic process we will do everything we can to starve the people of Chile. What we suggest you do instead is to kidnap the chief of staff of your army because he is in favor of the constitution, and then have a military coup and overthrow the government so that Mr. Allende, whom we find not acceptable, will not come to power." That is the kind of covert operation that I object to, and I submit that it is the kind of covert operation which in fact the CIA has been conducting in very many countries throughout the world.

Cline:

That is the kind of covert operation that I do not support either. That kind of covert operation in Chile in 1970 and

1971 was laid on by President Nixon and Dr. Henry Kissinger without consultation with much of the intelligence community. I know because I was the Director of Intelligence in the State Department at the time, and I know many intelligence people regretted it. That is the kind I'd like to get away from. The kind of intelligence operation that I would like to support is the financial assistance and the informational assistance to newspapers and to public opinion media in Chile in 1963 and '64, to support the Democratic Christian effects of Mr. Frei who undoubtedly then and in the 1970's was the most popular man in Chile. If Frei had not been ineligible for reelection I am sure that Allende would never have been elected. The CIA program was to try to create a center moderate parliamentary government in Chile with a progressive social and economic program. It did pretty well for several years. That program was discontinued in the late sixties, and then what I consider personally to be a rather misbegotten belated attempt to do something in Chile was laid on by the White House.

This leads me to my final remark. The CIA is an instrument of policy in the covert action field. If you don't like the way instruments are used, change the people who are using them, but don't destroy the instrument.

Colby:

I think it is important to clarify the record about Chile in terms of what the CIA did not do. Senator Church and I differ a little on this approach, but nonetheless I think there is a contention to be made that with one exception, which was directed personally by the President, the CIA's program in Chile over many years was essentially one of supporting democratic forces. This started many years ago, and it terminated in 1973. Our effort during that time was to sustain democratic forces, parties, groups, media, through a period in which they were being pressured and suppressed by a government which represented thirty-six percent of the voters. That government was denounced by the Congress, by the Supreme Court and by the Comptroller General of Chile as operating outside the constitution.

We made a conscious decision that we did not want to bring about a military coup, and we separated ourselves from the leaders of the military who did lead the coup. Our policy was to look forward to the elections of 1976, which we hoped the democratic forces would win.

We had nothing to do with the 1973 overthrow by the army which, as was accurately said, we had always appraised as being perhaps one of the most constitutional armies in Latin America. But they were driven to the wall in the summer of 1973 and they, on their own, as they have testified themselves, and I think our evidence indicates, carried out the coup that overthrew Mr. Allende.

I think this is important because there is a total misconception in terms of what the CIA's program and policy were. This misconception stemmed from some misinterpretations of testimony I gave in 1973 to an executive session of our oversight committee, which was then repeated, and words were put into my mouth characterizing our program as one of "destabilization." That word I never used, and it was not our program. Our program essentially was one of supporting the democratic forces during a period in which they were put under a great deal of pressure.

Church:

Since Mr. Colby and I are in some disagreement on the Chilean policy, I would like to have just a word. In the first place it is, of course, true that Mr. Allende was elected by a plurality of vote, not a majority. It is also true that Mr. Nixon was elected by a plurality of the vote, not a majority. Both Presidents, Mr. Nixon and Mr. Allende, were legitimate Presidents under the constitutional system of each country. In every case in the previous political history of Chile, when a candidate got a plurality of the vote he was the candidate who was chosen by the Congress as having received the largest number of votes and he then became the President. That has been the practice in accordance with their constitutional system.

It is also true that Mr. Allende's government, for which I hold no brief—I thought it was a dreadful government—moved toward curtailing freedom in Chile, but not so far as to declare opposition parties unlawful. They continued to function. The basic institutions of the government continued to function. There were municipal elections; people continued to vote. And when you compare the amount of democracy that still lived under Allende, who did believe in the constitutional system, to what succeeded him in the terrible bloodbath that brought on the present fascist government in Chile, there was an awful lot of freedom still left even under Allende.

Finally, Mr. Colby says that we were just trying to strengthen democratic forces and that the CIA's work was in the direction of trying to help parties that wanted to keep Chile democratic. But the single exception was to overthrow Allende, after he had been elected, by a military coup d'état. That's a mighty big exception, and to do it they had to remove the one man who stood in their way, who may just have been sufficiently influenced by West Point to believe that the army of Chile was not entitled to displace the decision of the Chilean people as to what kind of government should exist in their country. So everything we did was wrong, from start to finish.

Even though we did not have a hand in the final overthrow of the Allende regime, our participation and our effort to destroy that regime from the outset and our participation in every kind of activity to undermine it in the years that followed inevitably led to the uprising and the bloodbath and the kind of regime that followed. We've gotten the blame for it, and all over South America our capacity to exert moral leadership has been drastically weakened.

That is the whole problem with this covert business. You know, the President of the United States is not Caesar, and the Western Hemisphere is not a colony of the United States, and it is not the right of Washington to intervene and decide for other people what kind of government they shall have.

We once knew that. We once practiced it. And those were the days when we were the most respected country in the world. Let's get back to that.

Morgan:

I thought Senator Church's remarks were quite appropriate. Belief in the United States has been drastically weakened, and weakened also among ourselves. We ourselves are the doubters because we know the truth, and we can rectify that. We can't do it, however, with some sort of murky liberalism that says there are two sides to everything and no absolutes. You know, if Moses had gone to the Harvard Law School and spent three years on a staff on Capitol Hill he would have written the Ten Commandments with three exceptions and a savings clause.

The hallmark of liberalism in America is apparently set by the editorial pages of the *Washington Post* and *The New York Times* and the *Los Angeles Times*. I have nothing against the editor of the *Washington Post*; he used to be with the Agency. And the editor of *The New York Times*, he used to be with OSS, and the Chairman of the Board of the Times-Mirror Corporation used to be on the Foreign Intelligence Advisory Board.

Mott:

My second question follows on my first and it is a troubling one. Though we may admit to a CIA covert or overt operation that breaks the laws of another nation, I am troubled about the direct political support with dollars and advice that we give to so-called—by somebody's definition, I'm not sure whose—democratic elements. I think all of us here would find it rather obnoxious if it were learned that the American Independent Party, George Wallace, or Ronald Reagan were supported by some fascist regime, by Franco, or what have you. It would be obnoxious if we learned that the campaign of Gene McCarthy or George McGovern were financed by the Soviet Union. We have laws against that. We respect the integrity of the political process at home. But can you condone the notion that we shouldn't respect it abroad and that we ought to intervene with advice and money, overtly or covertly, in any other nation. I know the answer to that question is not simple. The French, because of their aid during the American Revolution, did help us get where we are today.

Church:

I think this is the hardest question that has been asked, and the best. I think on principle there's no way that you can defend a covert undertaking by the United States to finance a political party or a political movement in some foreign country. It is easy to understand that because all you have to do is turn it around and ask yourself, would we find it acceptable for a foreign country to do that here? If anybody in this room thinks that we would find it acceptable for a foreign government secretly to finance a political movement in this country, I would be very surprised. And of course, if that isn't fair play for them to do to us, it isn't, it logically follows, fair play for us to do it to them.

Having said that, I haven't adequately answered the question because there is another element in the picture. And that element is a very persistent and aggressive Soviet

Union, which is, I suppose, less troubled by such moral questions than we are. The Soviet Union has intervened very actively, has contributed a good deal of money and other kinds of help on behalf of political movements within foreign countries, namely, communist movements. I would say no, we have no right to intervene in Canada or in Mexico or in any other country that is handling its own affairs without undue foreign intervention. But if you get a little country like Portugal, let's say, that the Soviet Union decides it's going to turn communist by a massive covert penetration and wants to do it by forcibly imposing a minority party upon the will of eighty-four percent of the Portuguese people, then you've got to ask, in that situation, is it a permissible thing for the United States to step in and try to give a hand to the large majority of Portuguese who are trying to achieve and preserve a free government? When you add that dimension to it, I think then there are times, as after the Second World War when the restoration of democratic government in Western Europe was a covert action, when such covert action falls within the lines of permissible activity, given the zeal and determination of the Soviet Union to intervene covertly in the political affairs of those very countries. But I draw the line very narrowly, and I say it is permissible only in such situations when it conforms to our traditional values as a nation. It is a very tough question, and that's the best answer I can give.

Mott:

Part of the answer leads me to think that perhaps the CIA should engage George Gallup to take a poll before intervening, if ever the situation is that vague. Only in the clearest cases could I find any justification for this.

I agree with an earlier comment that the greatest difficulty is that for years and years and years now, aiding democratic movements isn't what we've been doing in our covert operations. We have been doing just the opposite. We have actually thought that it was our mission to be the sentinel of the status quo in the world. And that is a world largely in ferment, largely still controlled by despotic governments, repressive governments, rotten governments of one kind or another. Covert action on our part has been to keep these governments in place, as though we could squelch the volcanoes of revolution that have to occur in much of the world. That has put us on the wrong side. It has made covert action completely contrary to our traditional principles, and it has undermined the prestige and the good name and reputation of the United States throughout the world. It's been the wrong policy, absolutely the wrong policy.

Cline:

I want to make a couple of brief remarks about other speakers' statements. I think that Mr. Mott's second question was answered beautifully by Senator Church, and I subscribe to that answer. But I would like to make it a little clearer. Ask the question this way: Supposing in a country like Portugal it was absolutely clear that thirteen percent of the society, through control of military force and the propaganda organizations of the country, was going to establish a one-party dictatorship under Soviet or some other totalitarian society's control. Would you walk away from that problem?

A great deal of the comments here have suggested yes, we should. I think that that represents what I call a Kitty Genovese complex. You all remember that poor woman in New York who was stabbed to death, slowly and painfully, while everybody else shut their doors and windows and didn't even call the police. I think we do have a moral responsibility in the world to try to support the kind of open societies that Senator Church spoke about. Maybe we haven't supported all the right ones; that's a policy decision. But I think we ought to support them.

Now the second point: The reason we suffered that traumatic blow at Pearl Harbor is that we were relying on the Neutrality Act to prevent us from getting involved in the disorders of the world, and we didn't have any central intelligence system to tell us when dangers were approaching. We went naked into World War II, intelligence-wise, and if we go naked into the conflicts of the next decade in the same way we will suffer similar disasters.

Colby:

We always face the possibility that some country or other may develop an independent nuclear capacity in the next ten to twenty years. I don't think we have to wait until their bombs land on us. We really ought to be taking some steps to insure that if nuclear capacity is developed at all—and maybe we can get them not to develop it—it should be in hands friendly to us rather than hostile to us.

The framework of covert action has always been the interests of the United States as a sovereign power in a world in which there are a number of other sovereign powers. We have not been on an ideological crusade. This explains why we have responded, essentially, to threats by another great power and its local satraps to extend their power and strength. This explains also why we have not conducted an ideological crusade to overthrow right-wing governments around the world. Right-wing governments have not constituted a threat to the United States. If they should, presumably we will do something about it.

Halperin:

As Mr. Colby has just made clear, it is absolutely no accident that the United States did not intervene on the side of democratic forces because, precisely as he says, what we have been interested in is our own national interest, as we define it. And that means that a Portuguese government which for twenty-five years is a repressive totalitarian regime is totally acceptable to the U.S. It is acceptable because it gives us the bases we want and cooperates with us in our military security. We become concerned with Portugal not because we suddenly become interested in democracy there and worry about the democratic forces. We become concerned with Portugal because we fear that a government will come to power which will not give us those bases and which will not cooperate with us in defining security as we define it. That inevitably means that we end up supporting safe regimes which are right-wing military dictatorships, because left-wing governments have threatened to become antagonistic to us or friendly to the Soviet Union.

If we are going to intervene in consistence with our ideals, we can do it openly. It's not a secret to anybody in the world that the United States is intervening now in Portugal. It's no secret that the Western European democratic parties are intervening in Portugal. It's not a secret that the communist parties are intervening in Portugal. There is no reason why that cannot be a publicly argued decision in the U.S. There is no reason why the President cannot ask for funds for that, just as he asks for funds for other purposes. And then we can debate in this country whether we want to give aid to those people. Where the thing is consistent with our ideals, then we can do it openly. We only have to do it covertly when the President knows that he can't get the support because it's contrary to Congress's view of our political interests or contrary to our ideals.

Church:

I agree very much with what Mr. Halperin has just said. It seems to me we have to draw a distinction between what we view as our national interests, our strategic interests, our economic interests, whatever they may be. We have interests in the world. In pursuing those interests through normal diplomatic channels and in normal ways we must accept governments as they come. The dictatorships, the democracies, the despotisms, the communist states—we have to accept these governments as they come and deal with them as best we can. We can protect our strategic interests with open alliances, even though those alliances may be, in some cases, with governments which we would not approve. But when it comes to covert action, secretly undertaken to manipulate events within foreign countries, then I'm afraid that within the last twenty years we've been far more controlled by our fears than we have been by our faith in our own system. Our fear has been that revolution in itself is a threat to us because the Communists somehow will emerge from the revolutionary process in control of the world and we will slowly sink in a great red sea.

It is that fantasy of the Cold War, that obsession, which we must throw aside. We've got to remember that 5,000 years of history teaches us that this world is much too big, people are much too tough, the philosophies of various religions and cultures are much too diverse for any one system or one philosophy, let alone one national government, to control it all. So let's get back to our faith in our own system and never intervene on any other basis but that.

III

THE COLD WAR AND
THE DOMESTIC ECONOMY

Mayor Tom Bradley opens Part III of this volume with an eloquent plea that we not "abandon our own people while trying to buy the hearts and minds of others." Our priorities, he says, must not "relegate homegrown problems to second place." Today, as Mayor Bradley sees it, "foreign policy is hardly distinguishable from domestic policy." The failure of foreign policy and national security planners to consider the home front as well as that abroad, the Mayor charges, is responsible for the plight of our cities and has produced "a crisis of confidence" in American institutions which adversely affects national security. The Mayor calls for "a Marshall plan for the cities" to promote urban recovery in the United States just as the original Marshall plan promoted economic recovery in Europe.

Professor Seymour Melman's thesis, argued with facts and figures, is that military spending of the magnitude of the Cold War budgets not only produces inflation but also, because it does not contribute to consumable goods and services, unemployment. In the process, he says, our basic productive capacity has been undermined. From 1946 to the present, according to Professor Melman, our military spending has amounted to "sixty-three percent of the value of everything that is man-made and therefore replaceable on the surface of the United States." He traces the financial plight of New York and other cities in large part to "net capital outflows" resulting from taxes used to pay for military enterprises. In the last analysis, Professor Melman says, "the issue is plainly one of values," and he asks: "What kind of people do we want to be?"

Otis Graham urges a definition of national security which includes the well-being of Americans at home. He sees certain institutional developments that could help make this possible but feels they are neither adequately implemented nor coordinated. Any realistic military planning, he declares, must consider "those domestic foundations of American strength which have been taken for granted and allowed to weaken while we defended our shores against an outside invader who has never come and may not be required for our defeat."

National Security and the Plight of Our Cities

Tom Bradley

When Pope John issued his mighty encyclical *Pacem in Terris,* it was to become an historical document filled with optimism and opportunity for a world locked in prisons of suspicion and gloom. His simply written moral message produced rays of hope which helped thaw the Cold War mentality.

The fact that we are meeting at this convocation sponsored by the Fund for Peace and the Center for the Study of Democratic Institutions is high testimony to the lasting influence of Pope John's prescription for Peace on Earth.

We meet at a time when Beirut, Angola and Northern Ireland are bloody battlefields of suffering and despair. Each is a dateline of useless death and destruction. Each is a reminder that we still haven't learned how to live at peace with one another.

In this country, we have our own battlefields: America's cities. In any one of thousands of cities and towns across this land, each day is a struggle for survival; each hour brings us closer to the brink. We only have to

Tom Bradley is Mayor of Los Angeles.

look at New York as a practical lesson. But it could be Boston or Cincinnati, Detroit or Dallas, San Francisco or my city, Los Angeles.

Uncertainty of direction in federal policies—policies governing economics, energy and spending, to name a few—has meant that America's cities are being asked to do more and more. But the simple truth is that we've been asked to attack the problems without enough strategic support, and casualties have been enormous.

We all know what they are: too few policemen on our streets, too few firemen, inadequate services, strikes and lockouts, haphazard education, debilitating unemployment and so on.

We who fight this battle daily have longed for peace and pleaded that this nation set straight its priorities. The war in Indo-China ended, and we hoped that the billions which were spent in financing it would be shifted to plans for peace, to help with the domestic problems in the cities and towns across America. But, of course, there was no "peace dividend." A policy of increased military and foreign aid expenditures was perpetuated and the problems of inflation worsened.

Our cities have become the victims of a decade of preoccupation with Vietnam. And after Vietnam, Watergate and oil prices once more drew the nation's attention away from the plight of urban America.

It is in our cities where fiscal deficits force cutbacks in fire and police protection. It is in our cities where the lines of jobless workers stretch the longest. It is in our cities where families are desperate to flee apartments they share with rodents. And it is in our cities where hundreds of thousands of homes have already been abandoned.

The mayors of our cities—playing the role of domestic statesmen or diplomats—are on the front line. We see the anger and the frustration. We face the legitimate demands for clean sidewalks, for streets where people can walk without fear, for schools, for jobs in which men and women can earn decent wages and for a climate of progress that attracts rather than repels investments.

There is something wrong when pleas for emergency aid to cities do not bring response. There is something wrong when our vital requests are answered by White House vetoes. And there is something wrong when our voices do not produce a congressional consensus to override those vetoes.

The federal government seems to understand inflation only when it comes to the defense budget.

But where is the same understanding when it comes to the need to provide services in our cities? Where is there a sense of understanding that the security of the people in Boston, Birmingham and Baltimore is not only determined by the magnitude of our missile and submarine power, but by the strength of our police and fire forces, by the quality of our schools and medical care, and by the adequacy of housing and employment?

If the federal government can keep pace with inflation for the Defense Department, then it can keep pace with inflation for the cities of America.

If the federal government can maintain the U.S. commitment to foreign defense budgets, then it can maintain a national commitment to social progress in our cities.

If the federal government can listen to the pleas of foreign heads of state and to our own generals and admirals, then it can listen to the pleas of its mayors and citizens.

We are making a grave error if we continue to allow our cities and towns to suffocate or stagnate while trying to cover all our bets in the international game of economic roulette.

Today, foreign policy goes far beyond the traditional bounds of strategic weapons, military alliances or economic expansion. Today, the substance of foreign policy is hardly distinguishable from what is called "political" policy, or perhaps more important, what has commonly been called "domestic" policy.

On the home front, we must come to recognize and deal with the intricate relationships which are becoming more and more complex. Such issues as oil, food, unemployment, abandoned central cities and the environment are so interrelated that they sometimes overwhelm us. Recent events have shown that trying to distinguish between them, or trying to deal with them as separate issues, is inconsistent with reality.

When American consumer interest in the price of bread or soybeans conflicts with this country's relations with Russia or Japan; when our Middle East policy raises imported oil prices from $7 billion in 1973 to $24 billion in 1974 or results in long lines at our gas stations; when the price of tuna on the West Coast is tied to the actions of Peru or Ecuador—then the relation between foreign and domestic concerns is direct and difficult. This much is clear: international forces in today's world have a direct impact at the grocery store and on unemployment lines, whether they are in Detroit, Rome or elsewhere.

It is evident that foreign and domestic policies cannot operate in a vacuum. This country plainly does not have the wherewithal to be all things to all nations. And our priorities cannot relegate homegrown problems to second place. An indelible domestic element should become the foundation of our foreign policy, without abandoning our long-standing charitable tradition of sharing our wealth to provide humanitarian assistance where needed around the globe.

We must ask ourselves, then: How much military and foreign aid do we need and can we afford, consistent with our social obligations at home and security needs abroad? Many in the military and foreign policy establishments, concerned as they are with such things as the "balance of power" and meeting "potential threats to our vital interests," seem to imply sometimes that all important factors affecting this nation's foreign policy emanate only from abroad.

Sometimes those establishments fail to take into serious account the necessary constraints imposed by the wishes of citizens in a democracy and the pressing needs at home, particularly in urban America.

There is a need, I believe, for fundamental change in developing policy to meet both domestic and foreign interests. The need for change is symbolized by the attitude of a national administration which leaves New York City teetering on the brink of bankruptcy one week, and in the next week announces its $4.7 billion foreign military and security assistance plan. Is this the new American way? Are we willing to abandon our own people while trying to buy the hearts and minds of others? I hope not.

I would oppose a return to isolationism as vigorously as I call for recognition of our domestic needs. The realities of our world dictate a life-line role for national interdependence and for reconciliation with old antagonists. The American people understand and accept the economic ties of the nations of the world, but they are increasingly calling for reordered priorities in a way that cannot be dismissed as a short-lived phenomenon in the wake of Vietnam.

What many want is a foreign policy which acknowledges not only the interdependence among nations, but also the interrelationship with local problems and economic cycles. They want a policy of friendship, built on trust and respect among nations, a policy which doesn't shift with every wind off the Syrian desert.

Twelve years ago in his *Pacem in Terris* encyclical, Pope John admonished us to replace porous foundations "upon which our present peace depends." His wisdom shines even brighter today. It's time for America to look inward.

With due respect to our foreign obligations, we must build a new structure of social justice to serve as a national policy framework for the cities and towns of this country. It should be a policy strong enough to overcome today's problems but flexible enough to meet tomorrow's challenges.

As for our short-term needs, permit me to take advantage of the holiday season and present you with a brief shopping list for a vigorous urban America.

First, we need a firm national policy of full employment. Programs to meet this commitment should include public service jobs, new housing construction, community redevelopment and special economic assistance for hard-pressed areas.

Next, we need to expand the general revenue-sharing concept to allow for specialized aid where needs exist.

We need new methods for controlling crime and administering justice.

We need new and better transportation systems, with urban mass transit a primary goal.

And we need stability in the urban money markets. The uncertainty surrounding New York City's financial troubles has already cost other local governments untold millions of dollars in higher interest rates.

Beyond these immediate steps, I want to mention several propositions to reduce future shock.

For a number of years now, I have been interested in strengthening local economies so that they might withstand the trauma of change. My interest was kindled and kept ablaze because Southern California—particularly its aerospace, defense and auto industry—is especially susceptible to cyclical and structural recessions. In response to this, I proposed a few years ago the development of a Joint Economic Revitalization and Productivity Board.

This federally-appointed local board would direct innovative pilot studies and recommend ways of revitalizing, diversifying and redirecting the economy to care for basic community needs. With a board comprised of local representatives of industry, labor and finance, people with first-hand knowledge and daily involvement would help put together programs which have practical application.

The potential of this kind of mechanism is boundless. Areas like Los Angeles or Detroit, which are dependent on recession-sensitive industry, are ideally suited to serve as prototypes for this kind of economic conversion. Investments in such areas would be minimal because of their high concentrations of facilities and skilled workers. Local reconversion efforts, focused on invigorating sluggish economies, are long overdue.

When this concept was first proposed, both the Departments of Labor and Commerce expressed support, but rapid shifts of personnel in Washington stymied final action. I trust its fate will be more positive this time. Though I wish the situation were different, there is no better time than now, with unemployment high and the economy strung out by inflation, to formulate this kind of progressive action.

Another idea I would like to see promoted further is the concept of an urban recovery program — a Marshall Plan for the cities, if you will. Just as billions of dollars in post-war economic aid for Europe was spent in the two decades following World War II, the same sort of investment should now be made at home. The goal of such an ambitious program should be to recapture the attractive, healthy lifestyle which made this country thrive. To this end, urban recovery should become a high national priority.

We must act, and act swiftly and effectively in this recovery. If not out of humane motives, then out of real concern for the very survival of our institutions in the cities.

As a nation, we have to develop the capacity to manage our cities so that we don't forfeit the tremendous investments of time, money and energy in our great metropolitan areas. Restoring them, of course, is not a simple proposition. Years of neglect, waste and inaction cannot be swept away overnight. While it won't be easy, it is not an impossible dream. But we must begin now.

To be sure, our ability to solve urban problems depends greatly on our ability to wrestle with and overcome such problems as inflation, recession and crime. But perhaps the most difficult task before us—in promoting city living again as an attractive lifestyle—is the reshaping of the national psyche which developed during this country's years of affluence.

This nation's technology explosion during the twentieth century produced better living standards for millions.

Along with our growing affluence, though, we developed a tendency to become a disposable society. We use something for a while and then simply toss it away. Every day we throw away untold thousands of disposable cans and bottles, disposable lighters, cameras and even disposable clothing and furniture. In our affluent technological society, we have created the dubious art of producing something, using it up, throwing it away and simply replacing it.

This disposable trend is even reflected in a too common philosophy about our cities—particularly our central cities: Get out fast. Don't look back.

At the first sign of deterioration and blight, there is the tendency to pick up and move out, to run away instead of facing up to the challenge of rejuvenating, of restoring life to old, dying portions of American cities.

We must now frankly ask ourselves if it is in our best interests to continue the wasteful practice of quick use and rapid disposal. I, for one, am convinced that we cannot afford the luxury of throw-away cities any longer. We cannot afford to turn our backs on our gasping cities and run to the newest suburbs.

Reversing this trend, bringing about a change in this throw-away-cities philosophy, is the key, I believe, to the salvation of the American metropolis. And by salvaging cities, we will at the same time take a giant step toward regaining some all-around national stability.

Government's inability—at all levels—to address key national issues such as I have mentioned fosters a lack of overall public confidence, a decline in optimism about the future and even a drop in aspirations. I am sure this attitude has had an impact on the economy and on how government is perceived abroad and here at home.

Certainly the performance of government leadership is vital to a democracy's ability to withstand accelerating, bewildering, unnerving change, particularly when the belief in progress for its own sake becomes another casualty of our crowded, diverse existence. It is this failure of government to perform the vital role—particularly in dealing with the impact of our foreign policy decisions on our economy—of conducting an educational dialogue that makes the choices unclear and the future incomprehensible. This is what we now see reflected in the crisis of confidence.

No single law or leader, no simple slogan or dramatic act can, by itself, renew the loss of trust. But a concerned, continuing effort by government at all levels to explain the complexities of policy, to bring the people into the process of evaluating alternatives, to admit indecision when evidence is inconclusive, to promise only what can realistically be expected is the only way to revitalize the democratic system and restore the public's confidence.

As we move into the third century of this Republic, I believe this nation must return to its founding tradition of dialectic democracy, a democracy where action is determined by forthright discussion and the synthesis of ideas.

So now we face tomorrow. And it is up to those with faith in themselves to speak with a clear voice and to act with a strong heart and a clear conscience. It is up to all of us to serve this present age well so that the crises which confuse our future become converted into clear options from which we can choose our tomorrow: a day of renewed hope, a day of truth and sincerity, a day of freedom and justice for all and a day of peace, within ourselves and with others.

The Economic Crisis

Seymour Melman

I have ten points to make about our economic crisis.

1. Economic instability is as old as industrial capitalism. The source of instability was always found in the superstructure of industrial capitalism, so that it was possible to adjust money flow, spending, and interest rates and thus evoke a new economic activity. Now that is no longer possible, and that gives the present economic crisis its special character.

2. The whole range of conventional economic theory is now failing. In the center, the understanding is that if you have a recession or a depression, you can terminate it with substantial government spending. But now we have both. On the right, the characteristic understanding is that inflation can be traded off for unemployment. Now we have both. On the left, the understanding is that one will have either economic stagnation or a war economy. And now we have both.

3. Something new is present in the economy which is not accounted for by the previous array of ideas. This new factor is a military activity which is important and dur-

Seymour Melman is Professor of Industrial Engineering, Columbia University.

able, and in which military products are counted as ordinary economic end products. This swells the calculated national income and the calculated national product, because even though military products have no economic use value (they cannot be consumed and they cannot be used for further production), being money-valued, they are counted along with everything else. So the increase in military production increases what is ordinarily called economic growth. This new factor erodes and undermines the production capability which has long been present in the American economy and society. It was always assumed that this country could pay the highest wages in the world and that this would be offset by sufficient mechanization and organization of work so that, at appropriate productivity levels, we would have high wages along with economical and quality products. Now our ability to do that is being eroded in one industry after another.

4. In industrial capitalism, technology and capital are controlling categories. Now who controls? From 1951 to the present day, the budget given to the Pentagon every year has exceeded in size the after-tax profits left in the hands of all corporations put together. Concerning technology, since World War II, between seventy-five and eighty percent of the federal government's research and development activities (which dominate those fields) have been in military and related technology. The consequence is visible. I will give two examples: (a) The United States now operates the oldest stock of metal-working machinery of any industrial country in the world; (b) in 1966, for the first time in the history of such records, the average price of electricity rose instead of declined. It rose because of the technology and the capital the federal government had put into nuclear and related enterprises in which the government and military establishments are so heavily involved.

5. One of the consequences of this is massive and durable unemployment. Because of the spending of the bil-

lions of dollars each year by the military, fewer jobs are generated per billion dollars spent than there would be if that money had been spent in nonmilitary ways. Nonmilitary expenditure for further production continually renews itself; it makes itself more productive. None of that happens on the military side. In military expenditure, there is no marginal productivity of capital whatever. As a result, we suffer the relative loss of 840,000 jobs each year on the average. Also, concentration on the military together with the depletion of numerous civilian industries has made investment in the latter less attractive to holders of capital. So investors go abroad. In the 1960s there was an avalanche of capital outflow from this country, and today there are more than four million fewer jobs in the United States, on direct count, because of the concentration of capital and related resources on the military and because of the induced outflow of capital, mostly to Western Europe and Canada. If you make even the most modest estimate of further unemployment effects from that core group, allowing for a multiplier not of 2.8, as many economists do, but only of one, then you cannot escape the conclusion that eight million jobs have been lost in the American economy due to the military enterprise.

6. Regarding money, we have been taught for so long to have faith in the value of the dollar that we have ignored the fact that the value of the currency is associated with what currency represents. Having spent one and a half trillion dollars in all manner of resources for military purposes since World War II, there has been an inescapable deterioration in the meaning of that currency. Thus, a permanent war economy is also necessarily an inflation-inducing economy.

7. Concerning the cities, allow me to be parochial and talk about my town, New York City. The mostly unseen and hardly discussed factor in New York's crisis is not the productivity of the sanitation men or whether there are too

many clerks in the mayor's office. The unseen factor is the relation between taxes taken from the citizens of New York City and what comes back to them from the federal government. Some states gain richly from the activities of the federal government. They are the states which are priority locations for military industry and, in recent years, for military bases.

Now listen to the list of states that suffer net outflows of their resources, that is to say, those states whose capital (hence, purchasing power) is removed and transferred elsewhere to suit the priority purposes of the federal government, which means military purposes. The principal states experiencing that deficit are Delaware, Michigan, Illinois, New York, Ohio, Connecticut, Colorado, Minnesota, Indiana, Pennsylvania, Wisconsin, Missouri. Notice that every one of these states is a center of traditional civilian industry and operations. Every one of them is being ripped off. Every one of them is suffering the consequences of this extraction process.

There is wonderment about the condition of New York City. In the late 1960s the citizens of New York City experienced an estimated outflow of three billion, two hundred million dollars a year, more than enough to handle all the city's deficits, more than enough to cope with the economic development which was never accomplished for the citizens of New York. By 1973, that net outflow for the people of New York City was seven and a half billion dollars a year. The remarkable fact is the quality and scope of the services that successive mayors and city administrators of New York City have been able to provide despite the theft of their sustenance. The plain fact is that the federal government has not only taken from the "New York Cities" of this country, it has also given massive subsidies elsewhere, and not only to the military enterprise. There are subsidies to suburban home-building through tax-deductible interest, and subsidies to build fine transporation systems for the suburbs.

And there is an absence of subsidies in the big cities, as illustrated, for example, by our neglect of the elderly poor, and by the federal government's failure to cope with the drug traffic which helps to victimize hundreds of thousands of Americans.

The people of New York City are being forced to a lower standard of living in order to provide the capital and purchasing power the federal government requires for the military.

8. The issues of race and the issues of metropolitan development are joined in this country. They are one and the same. When the "Gerald Fords" of this country speak with contempt and disdain of the "New York Cities," they have discovered a new code word for contempt for an important segment of our countrymen. We should not tolerate it, not for a moment.

9. A crucial point in operating the current war economy is the prevention of any capability for converting from a military to a civilian economy, and the prevention of all planning, either at the national level or the local level, for achieving that conversion.

10. There is a massive conflict between many of our traditional ideologies and the reality all around us. Americans learned, they thought, that war brings prosperity because World War II seemed to end the Depression. But four years of that war and the ability to bring almost eighteen million new people into a military "labor force" was no model on which to forecast the consequences of thirty years of the permanent war economy we have had since the end of World War II. In those thirty years, the failure to innovate and to invest in the civilian economy is now bearing its bitter fruit. War does *not* bring prosperity. War brings destruction of every sort. We thought that military spending was good for economic growth. This is not true. Of course, military spending puts purchasing power in the hands of those who perform military services. But they contribute nothing of economic worth to the rest of the society. The consequence for the

whole community is a transfer of purchasing power along with a net reduction in real economic resources. The monies spent by the military from 1946 until now are equal to sixty-three percent of the value of everything that is man-made, therefore replaceable, on the surface of the United States. Only in that way can one understand what is otherwise inexplicable, namely, apparent economic growth for a quarter-century combined with massive decay in the great cities of our country. We are the only major industrial country of the world in which that is happening.

Finally, the issue is one of values, not numbers, and not this theory or that. The issue is: What kind of people do we want to be? Do we want to give heed to the human needs of human beings and to their desires to lead productive lives? Or will we continue to give heed to the idolatry of the nationalist symbols and give the military all the treasure and all the capital they ask for, without stint and without question?

National Security Begins at Home

Otis Graham, Jr.

Although all eras seem critical to those who live in them, the present moment can confidently be called critical in the discussion of national security policy. We are within reach of a new and larger conception of the idea of national security, just at the time that we are desperately in need of it.

Over a generation of Cold War a narrow definition of national security has led the United States to channel more than a trillion dollars into the building of an awesome arsenal of death and a military-industrial complex. But those years also produced a good deal of restlessness and questioning of the ongoing definition of how best to insure national security. Materials are now at hand, intellectually and politically, for a redefinition of how to make this country strong. It could not be more urgent to accomplish this redefinition, for in fiscal year 1975 the Nixon-Ford administration began a major expansion of military spending which was followed up in the fiscal year

Otis Graham Jr. is an Associate of the Center for the Study of Democratic Institutions and a Professor of History at the University of California at Santa Barbara.

1976 budget. Every indication is that military claims on the budget will be pushed upward again in 1977. The Pentagon has already started its annual alarm about Soviet power, and detente is everywhere under criticism. We must all sense that the country is not satisfied with its international strategies, and important decisions lie ahead.

The federal budget appears to be a unified document in that it is sewn together and published at one time. But, of course, among the many peculiarities of the American process of deciding upon the governmental agenda is the traditional separation of military from so-called domestic programs and budgetary claims. Foreign policy is one thing, domestic policy is another. The first in importance is foreign policy, for this involves national security with overriding claims, especially since 1941. So has run the operating assumption in American governmental circles. Intelligent people, of course, knew that there were reciprocal impacts between the international activities of this nation and the domestic condition. But there was no inclination in the process of making policy to try to take these reciprocal impacts seriously into account.

The operative division of military from domestic policies, deeply rooted since World War II, has in fact nonetheless collected questions and critics over the years. Let me select some illuminating examples. Harry Truman in 1949 perceived a relationship between resources and national security, and he appointed the Paley Commission on Materials Policy. Its historic report in 1950, while it was more shelved than read and focused too much on stockpiles of scarce materials, at least aired the insight that an essential basis of national security lay in natural resources, including the very fertility of the American soil.

It was about this time that intelligent conservatives such as Senator Robert Taft were perceiving the domestic impact of large military expenditures upon the size and power of the federal government, the size of the public relative to private sector, the power of the presidency as against branches with less direct responsibility for military and foreign relations. President Eisenhower came to share some of these concerns, and he struggled hard to contain defense spending, out of a primitive but important understanding that there are trade-offs in buying conventional military security, that security advanced by military spending on the one hand might weaken security somewhere on the home front.

Eisenhower's perception of the problem was lamentably simplistic. If the military budget were not contained, we would have socialism. That is a curious line of thought. One has heard it from the Ford administration in slightly different terminology. But Eisenhower's intuition that national security might be a broader concept than the Pentagon and the State Department allowed was thoroughly sound. And Eisenhower groped for institutional remedies, being more inclined toward administrative adjustments than to deep thought. He invited Secretary of the Treasury Humphrey to sit in with the National Security Council—that relatively new institution set up in 1947 to rationalize and formulate foreign policy. Ike expected him to speak up for frugality and a balanced budget, once a day. Apparently he did. Ike also ordered that every National Security Council paper have a financial appendix attached. In a crude but significant way, the idea of national security received a small balancing component on the domestic side.

The 1960's have been enormously educational along these lines, as Mayor Bradley has indicated. We appreciate so much that we did not formerly understand, partly because of riots, fuel and food shortages, partly because of books by people like Professor Melman, Richard Barnet, Ralph Lapp, William Proxmire and others.

We are well instructed in a painful school in the many interconnections and trade-offs between foreign and domestic life in this country. A web connects them all. A war is decided upon in faraway Vietnam and the resultant domestic political turmoil topples the President who decided upon it. The arms race is pursued by two liberal Presidents with singular fervor and financial generosity, and our cities deteriorate into foul air, traffic jams, violent crime, fiscal default. Research and development funds voted for space or nuclear weapons are now understood to come, like everything else, from a limited pool. Brains bought by the Pentagon are not available to do cancer research or work on mass transit. Our historic friendship with Israel is connected to long lines at the gas pumps. A State Department-encouraged sale of wheat to the USSR raises bread prices in Safeway.

More obviously than ever, what we do in international relations, especially what we spend upon the military, not only has a far reaching impact at home. Sometimes it has benefits like the alleged spillover in technology in the private sector. But more often it has cost in unmet civilian needs. And not only is this relatively simple truth more widely understood now in the public mind than ever before, but increasingly a more important extension of this truth is that national security policy is not foreign policy or defense policy, but potentially all policy. The domestic basis of national security is every day more appreciated. There is involved the natural resource base and its conservation, the human resources of the country and their conservation through health and educational expenditures, the transportation and communication infrastructure, the scientific and technological talent and, more important but less tangible, the very social cohesion of the nation. All of this affects national security, and that word must now be reclaimed from the five-sided building across the Potomac River, reclaimed from the House Armed Services Committee and broadened so that more voices are heard in formulating policies to insure national strength.

One gets a broader conception of the issue in part from administrative innovation. The traditional view of national security developed a big advantage in 1947 with the establishment of the National Security Council, which was charged "to advise the President with respect to the integration of domestic, foreign and military policies relating to national security." But it was a very closed group, that Council—the President, the Vice-President, the Secretaries of State and Defense. Others sat in: the heads of intelligence agencies, the military, and over in his visitor's chair and expected to say only one thing was the Secretary of the Treasury with his narrow but dogged insistence that a balanced budget and a sound dollar were also matters of national security. Time has brought attempts to broaden participation, to institutionalize the growing understanding in this country of the overlap between foreign and domestic policy.

Most of these institutional innovations, I must point out, came under Republicans, and rather recently. President Nixon in 1971 established the Council on International Economic Policy, to bring together many Cabinet heads, including the State Department along with Treasury and Transportation and the others. The State Department, the Treasury Department, the Defense Department and the Council of Economic Advisers were becoming more accustomed to interfering in each other's separate jurisdictions. This habit, and it is a desirable habit, was advanced again in 1972 when Peter Flanagan used interagency task forces to put together the Trade Relations Act of 1973. It was advanced in 1974 when President Ford put Secretary Kissinger on the Executive Committee of the Economic Policy Board on which the Secretary of the Treasury sits.

These are merely institutions. We don't know how well they work, But they are potentially places where, in a routine and well-staffed way, the trade-offs between the military definition of national security and the domestic aspects of national security may be clarified and intelligent choices made.

The Congress has helped by establishing at long last a procedure for looking at the budget as a whole, for working toward a ranking of priorities by comparing costs and benefits of proposed programs as well as one can. Institutionally, the old separation between military and domestic budget-making is breaking down.

Institutionally I'm not sure just where all this leads. The glaring absence of a coordinating supra-Cabinet place to focus and integrate domestic policies was apparently closed very late in the game in 1971 when President Nixon established the Domestic Council, with a staff as large as the National Security Council. Now presumably domestic issues are on an equal footing with foreign affairs. Both flow up to a central place for policy planning. Both policy centers have a staff. Actually they are not equal, however, for the National Security Council has the President's special affection and has that overriding charge to consider the domestic aspects of national security.

It would appear that at least one more institutional step is apparently required in the Executive Branch, an apex policy board where the trade-offs are finally clarified and choices made, where the Secretary of the Treasury may contend with the Generals for a sound dollar or more appropriations for narcotics control or whatever is close to his heart, where the Secretary of HUD may argue his perspective against that of the Secretary of State. Institutionally I don't know how this may be arranged. Nixon had an idea for a five-sided super-Cabinet, but this has its defects.

In any event, institutions of this sort in the executive branch are only so much machinery. They would leave out the many voices of consumers and others who must be expected to have their input in the national security policy discussion.

And we are still told by John Hersey in his series of articles, which is now a book based on hours spent with President Ford, that the President continues—like all his predecessors, let us be fair—to keep military and domestic discussions separate institutionally and presumably also in his head. Apart from electioneering, Ford, like all Presidents back to FDR, spends seventy or eighty percent of his time on foreign policy issues where Congress cannot easily frustrate him and where public opinion rewards seem to come so much more readily than on domestic issues.

Thus the job of recasting the national policy process so that national security will be viewed in its broadest sense is one that is not yet accomplished and is more urgent than ever. We must flush out into the open the hidden cost of every military expenditure, working perhaps along the lines of the National Security Budget proposed by the Joint Economic Committee in 1972. That was also the year of George McGovern's very interesting and ultimately unsuccessful effort to clarify for the public not just what the new missiles and ships could cost in dollars, but in alternative social purchases, schools, mass transit, education, the arts and environmental repair.

The stress we place on the domestic, economic and social factors involved in national security must be upgraded. The economic, social and environmental implications of defense policies must be clarified and debated and not remain obscure, as they now are. There must be a full discussion not only about the implications of war and preparations for war but also about those domestic foundations of American strength which have been taken for granted and allowed to weaken while we defended our shores against an outside invader who has never come and may not be required for our defeat.

IV

MILITARY SPENDING
AND UNEMPLOYMENT

In the discussion, Vernon Jordan and Willard Wirtz lend their voices to support the main points made by Messrs. Bradley, Melman and Graham. "Meaningful national security," Mr. Jordan says, must have full employment as a goal. He sees this, plus welfare reform, national health insurance and aid to cities as "absolutely essential to our internal strength." Mr. Wirtz emphasizes that public service employment, however needed in the short run, would hardly make a dent in the unemployment problem. He thinks technological change, among other things, contributes mightily to unemployment, and he believes there should be government assistance to people losing their jobs because of it. Professor Melman sees such a proposal as a proper part of planning for conversion to non-military production. He, Mayor Bradley and Mr. Wirtz are convinced that if we undertook now even the basic minimum of needed non-military projects a labor shortage would quickly develop. Answering a question from the audience, Professor Melman analyzes the amount in the military budget for "overkill." Other questions focus the discussion on federal-local relations, problems of tax reform and how well congressmen do their jobs.

Vernon E. Jordan, Jr.:

I want to express my thanks to my friend from Los Angeles, Tom Bradley, for a marvelously eloquent statement which suggests to me that we are getting better leadership from Los Angeles than we are from Washington.

While I am not by any means an expert in international affairs or foreign policy, one thing seems obviously clear to me and that is that true national security depends almost entirely upon our own internal strengths in this nation.

From that thesis I have a very difficult time trying to ascertain how in fact you build the kind of internal strength that leads to strong national security when in fact the Secretary of the Treasury himself has characterized the Food Stamp Program, a program feeding some 19 million people and another 40 million or so eligible, as a program of ripoffs and chiselers, while in fact a government study exists showing that the chiseling and ripping in the Food Stamp Program is really negligible. What I really believe is that upon reexamination you will find far

Vernon E. Jordan, Jr. is Executive Director of the National Urban League.

more ripoffs and chiseling in the defense spending program than in the Food Stamp Program.

I also have difficulty understanding how you can build true national security and not have a fully employed economy. I do not understand how you can have a true national security and not have a healthy citizenry, or true national security with a President who, in his State of Union address, says we cannot have national health insurance. I have difficulty with true national security where the citizenry is discriminated against, on the basis of race, color, and sex and where equal opportunity is not in fact a reality.

I have difficulty with the notion of strong true national security when employment in the black community borders at twenty-six percent and unemployment in the white community is at fifteen percent, and two out of every three teenagers in the ghetto cannot find work. I happen to believe that a fully-employed economy is in the best national interest, whether that interest deals with foreign policy or with national policy. I also believe that true national security is endangered when thirty percent of the black Vietnam veterans cannot find a job and a half million white Vietnamese veterans are standing in unemployment lines.

I also have difficulty believing that you can foster true national security when in fact our national leadership fosters an adversary situation between Los Angeles and New York or between the rest of the nation and one given city.

I further have real trouble with how you bring about a sound policy of national security when the CIA and the FBI carry on unconstitutional, illegal and unconscionable activities, whether they be against foreign nations or whether they be against our own citizens.

Therefore, it seems to me that a program of meaningful national security would be a program that would look at full employment as a national goal, that would look at welfare reform as something that needs to be brought about, that would see national health insurance, tax reform, public service employment, and aid to our American cities as absolutely essential to our internal strength, thereby giving us the kind of national security that we all need and are sure that we must have.

Question From The Floor:

Professor Melman, how much in the present military budget is for "overkill?"

Melman:

About twenty-five percent of the budget is for strategic forces. The strategic forces of the United States can now deliver more than 8,000 nuclear warheads to far away places—that's by the long-range bombers and the ICBM's, not counting any of the shorter-range planes and missiles. And it comes to be about forty-times overkill on every Russian city of 100,000 or over. Of course, we should take comfort because they can only do us in about twenty times over, so it shows who's ahead.

The other part of the military budget is for the so-called conventional forces. I'm afraid this language is grossly misleading because there's nothing conventional about them anymore, since they include cannon that can fire nuclear artillery shells and conventional forces that can plant nuclear land mines. And they include forces that can fire short-range missiles that are nuclear tipped. So there's no longer a real line of demarcation between the nuclear forces and a mass destruction effect and conventional forces with a lesser destruction effect. They both have massive destructive effects.

The strategic forces, however, are at least pro forma oriented to deterring an attack on the United States, though under Schlesinger renewed emphasis was given to the idea of trying to knock out an opponent by a first strike, called counterforce. The conventional forces are, of course, not designed to guard the shores of the United States, that project having become inoperable once several countries had nuclear weapons. So those forces are essentially designed to run Vietnam-type wars, of various kinds. And that accounts for the massive Air Transport Command facilities that the U.S. armed forces operates.

So if you want to know how much overkill is built in, the answer is, a lot. An enormous amount.

The only beginning of a serious attempt to get at the incredible abuse of the whole society that proceeds from the military budget was the imaginative attempt by George McGovern in 1972 to project a thirty-odd billion dollar cut in the military carried off in three years.

I think we tend to forget some of the things that have happened in the recent past and what they were supposed to signify for us. Remember the idea of the Peace Dividend after the Vietnam war? I'll bet not many of us here can even remember that in January, 1969, the last economic report of President Johnson included an important appendix on the economy after the end of hostilities in Vietnam. And included there was a rather detailed plan putting 39 billion 700 million dollars a year continuously into new civilian undertakings accounting for many of the desirable things that we're talking about here today.

Now if you price those things at present prices it will come to about 50 billion dollars a year of new civilian activity. That is the right order of magnitude for getting something constructive going in this country, for really reaching out to the employment problem, the cities' rebuilding problem and to the human needs of human beings in which we are so delinquent in many ways. So this was really worked out. It was done by a part of the President's Council of Economic Advisors, as they called in the Cabinet members and the staffs and asked them what blueprint-ready plans and ideas they had.

This stemmed out of the so-called War on Poverty

era. They produced a lot of detailed plans. Then these were pared down in size to make them very conservative, and it added up to 39 billion dollars a year. Of course, that agenda can be picked up and modified slightly, and it has validity today as much as it did some years ago. So there is not a lack of ideas or conceptions of how to do these things.

Willard Wirtz:

I would like to make two points especially. The first has to do with the employment situation and the unemployment figures. I tried to do some arithmetic as Mayor Bradley spoke. On the basis of assumed population, I think there must be about 250,000 unemployed in the Los Angeles area. As I understand it, there are about 7,400 jobs provided by the Comprehensive Employment Training Act—CETA. It is obvious that this is but a drop in the bucket. CETA applies to only about one-quarter of one percent of unemployment in Mayor Bradley's city.

I think we all had better begin to face up to the fact that talk about solving the unemployment problems of this country by public employment or public service programs is to talk about taking shortcuts across quicksand. Both parties in this country today are committing that error. I don't think it is a partisan policy.

Unemployment in this country is running about eight million. The maximum public service employment program that can be even conceived of as coming from the Congress would provide about 500,000 or 600,000 jobs. We aren't going to meet the problem that way, and we're putting off the questions that we have to face when we talk about that particular aspect of it.

I believe the complaint of Mayor Bradley and his colleagues goes a good deal deeper than that. It will not

Willard Wirtz is former Secretary of Labor.

be met by any public service employment program that will come out of Washington. It is time to face up to the fact that even those who speak well of the present condition talk about a continuing unemployment situation in this country that's going to run to about six to eight million people for the foreseeable future. And that is at any one time. Multiply that figure by two to get the unemployment that we can expect in any year, the number of people unemployed for the next five or six years, and then ask ourselves whether there are even the makings of an answer in the present situation. I don't believe there are.

I'm not inclined to put blame on the vicissitudes of political fortune. I'm inclined to look rather on an extraordinary confluence in time, which means that the technological revolution came to a peak when it did about the same time we had to face up to the facts of an exploding population. And about the same time that we ran out of some of the critical resources on which we have been depending and at about the same time that there was comparative peace in the world. I am inclined to ask whether any combination of the present ideas is going to meet that problem. I don't think it is.

We are going to have to face up to the fact that among other things Emperor Keynes has no clothes on, and the sooner we start thinking this whole thing through in terms of growth that is based on something other than those elements which are included in the measurement of the grossest national product in the world or in history, then we'll start finding the answers.

If we have within our own capacity and our human resources the capacities for a different kind of growth, then we will make it. And if we don't have those capacities, then we won't. I wish we'd stop talking about the shortcut answers of public service employment, although I would support every single public service employment program that came along, because it's absolutely necessary to meet the immediate situation. But until we start talking the other language we aren't going to develop those elements of economic strength which are essential to peace in the world.

My other point has to do with the obvious intention and the clear statement in the first part of Mayor Bradley's presentation. He points out so clearly that we are presently in a situation where the only answers we can hope for today must come from a reenlistment of the people of this country in the making of their own decisions. This loss of confidence in our institutions and our political process goes so deep today that anything we do about the Corrupt Practices Act and changing the election laws and so on isn't going to make a bit of difference. We're facing into another election with political credulity at absolute zero. Some corollary of Gresham's Law has so diminished democracy's critical currency, which is its dialogue, that none of us any longer knows how to distinguish between truth and falsehood in the political discourse, and we don't believe our representatives. That is the short and simple truth of it.

I hear Mayor Bradley saying that until we bring into the act, in one way or another, the people themselves, we're not going to find an answer to this problem. The awfulness of it is that if through some miracle the whole political process should be cleansed overnight, so that tomorrow morning every career servant in this town wakened as a model of public service and competency, and every politician a candidate for sainthood, we wouldn't believe a word of it. We are at the point where unless we are brought back into this decision-making, we are not going to believe the process.

I believe as fully as the Mayor in the decentralization today of authority. I believe in it because it seems to me that it is only at the local community level that there is the opportunity to bring people again back into the decision-making processes of this country. That's the only place we can do it, and that's the reason for the argument.

Bradley:

It seems to me that the comments made by Secretary Wirtz point to another facet of this problem. He is so right. CETA is really just a drop in the ocean. It doesn't even begin to meet our needs. But we're grateful for it because it did take 7,400 people off the unemployment lines at a critical point in our history.

There is another facet to this whole thing. I don't have the figures at my fingertips, but the amount of unemployment insurance which we are paying every year is mounting so rapidly that it just seems to me that we've got to begin to stop and take a look at that whole process.

It just doesn't make any sense to me. We have simply got to take a new look at it and to strike out in a new direction.

Wirtz:

Our annual bill for unemployment insurance is about $20 billion, although I would be subject to correction on this.

Melman:

May I add a further note on that. Earlier I noted that were there to be a 50 billion dollars a year new civilian investment operation, there would be a massive increment of new jobs. Because it would be civilian investment and economically productive it would have a considerable multiplier effect. Without dealing with any of the details, let me simply report that a number of colleagues and I have found that were there a turn in this direction we would face a labor shortage and especially a labor shortage in skilled productive occupations through at least the end of the century. The notion that this country doesn't have useful work to do is a desperately dangerous myth, a piece of self-deception, a kind of defeatism, and participates in helping to justify the present use of the collective resources of this society.

One of the hats I wear is that of National Co-Chairman of SANE, a peace organization. One of our priority issues is to encourage the development of constructive thinking and finally, we hope, legislation, to cope with economic conversion and civilian emphasis on production. I think that you, Mr. Mayor, in particular, in Los Angeles, with the problem of unemployment and also with the adjacent problems of military industry, are very much in a position where these matters touch really all the vital elements of future policy for yourself and your colleagues. I would like earnestly to invite your attention to and participation in an effort to formulate and sponsor appropriate legislation for conversion from military to civilian economy with a collateral effort to "go civilian" in a really serious way in this society.

Question From The Floor:

What about the impact of technology on the economy?

Wirtz:

The question involves the broader question of what we should do about technological progress of one kind or another if it means the loss of jobs. It does seem to me this is a problem we have to face up to, and I would make only two points about it. I would start the approach to the future on the clear basis that anybody who loses his job as a consequence of progress will be paid for that loss on exactly the same basis as we pay an individual who owns property which is taken over under eminent domain for the public use because of the needs of progress. I would see to it, to begin with, that no individual was penalized by the loss of his or her job, that any individual losing a job as a consequence of progress gets paid for it at its full value.

And I would make one other suggestion. That is that it would be the greatest mistake in the world to assume that we are running out of things to do in this country so that we must try to hang onto the things we already have. That's the most awful thing that could enter our minds. We're not running out of things to do; there is plenty to do if we would simply make one change, which would be to move from our present obsession of driving to work each morning and home each afternoon in each year a bigger and bigger car to give each of our egos a larger and larger satisfaction, driving in and out across concrete cobwebs that are beginning to choke every city in the country. If we could just give up the ego satisfactions of the automobile and turn to the mass transit, which is a necessity in this country, there would be a shortage of manpower to meet even that single change.

And then if you go on to think of all the other things that need to be done as far as education, health and all those things are concerned, there is much more to do. If we would start from the assumption that whoever is the particular victim of change is going to be protected fully in his job and then go on to the new agenda of possibilities, I think there is the broader answer to the question.

Melman:

I would like to supplement Secretary Wirtz's remark about the importance of backstopping people in periods of technological change so that the worker shouldn't bear the brunt of unemployment under those conditions. I think there is an interesting possibility of joining essentially a national insurance system to carry the burdens of technological change, of job change, with the kind of program that is needed for seeing people through conversion from military to civilian economy.

For both types of situations, job change is an important part of the scene. Both types of situations need new capital investment to provide new job opportunities. Both types of circumstances can be dealt with by drawing on our years that were well tested in the famous G.I. Bill of Rights following the Second World War. Some minimum income guarantees, provision for job retraining, provision for relocating and so on, and the whole thing could be handled without new bureaucratic setups through the already existing offices, as for example those for the State Employment Services.

I am looking forward to the earnest effort of a number of Congressmen, such as Andrew Young, who are planning new legislation on the economic conversion matter during the next months. I hope it will be possible to confer with representatives of trade unions so that the issue of job conversion on the condition of technological change can be joined with this type of effort and both can be made part of giving a new, constructive future for many millions of our people.

Question From The Floor:

What assurances might there be that if we were to cut back in spending in the military area we would be able to attract capital investment in the civilian area?

Bradley:

I can only indicate to you that a host of activities at the municipal level badly need doing. Our cities are growing older; they need to be revitalized. The transportation systems desperately need our attention. Housing is already deteriorating and dying in our cities. Those two major areas alone would provide for enormous investment of capital and create millions of jobs. I think they would help not only to give us new hope but new vitality in this country. But these are only two of the simplest kinds of answers I could give you. There are just enormous opportunities for investment of capital in rebuilding this country. There is no shortage of opportunity or ideas.

Question From The Floor:

What is the significance of tax reform?

Bradley:

We've been so frustrated on this matter—we have been pushing for this idea for so long without any kind of real response that you almost give up. I think I've just about come to that point. We've tried it in our state, we've tried it as far as Congress is concerned. We simply haven't had a meaningful comprehensive tax reform that would meet the needs of the people of this country.

Let me just give you an example. We in the cities are stuck with regressive property taxes, our major source of revenue. It doesn't make any sense. At best it grows by about five or five and a half percent each year. But the cost of living is growing about 11%. So we're falling deeper into the hole every year because we're stuck with property taxes as a basis for revenue. And that's crazy; we've simply got to do something about it. You find me somebody in Sacramento who will do it, or somebody in Washington, and I'll hug them all day.

Question From The Floor:

Mayor Bradley, would you say more about your observation that Congressmen don't get home enough to understand local problems.

Bradley:

I wouldn't for a moment want to suggest that the Congress is filled with incompetent representatives. That in my judgment is not the fact. The complexity of their job today is so different than it was in earlier years. They are literally overwhelmed by the amount of work they have before them. If you were just to review the amount of paper work they're expected to try to assimilate, that would give you some idea of the nature of the demands upon them.

It is the kind of burden which they bear which prevents them not just from getting home but from being able to reach the variety of people to get input, to be able to give adequate time to listen to, whether it is city officials or somebody else from home who has an idea or wants to discuss problems with them.

Graham :

I don't think Congressmen do their job better than they did. I don't think they ever did their job very well. But there are some signs that are hopeful in the Congress. You don't want to get your hopes up very far, but the Budget Act is potentially profoundly important. They finally have established a rudimentary and apparently workable system of looking at the total picture of what they're appropriating. And there are some other innovations. The Office of Technology Assessment now promises to give Congressmen a little bit of that help that you were referring to that they need.

Another mistake was in reading the 1972 election as proving that we should never again as Democrats, let alone Republicans, pick a candidate who raises the radical issues and thus gets himself clobbered. In one way, the McGovern campaign, which tried to address the question of defense balance versus domestic needs and national priorities and the question of jobs and the welfare system, seemed to have been a tragic mistake. I think the tragic mistake really would be to read that election as meaning we should never again engage in that kind of fundamental discussion.

Jordan:

May I please address myself to the business about the Congress. I rather think that the issue is not their quality, nor do I think that the issue is that they are out of touch with home or that they are so overwhelmed. I think the basic issues, certainly with the House of Representatives, is that a term of two years is too short. You spend one year running and the next year preparing to run. It seems to me that this bicentennial year is probably a good time to reevaluate the term of the Congressmen.

The problem with the Senators is that the Senators are either protecting their seniority or running for President. That is also a fundamental issue that ought to be addressed, as well as, in my view, the issue of a one-term, six-year Presidency so we will not get the kind of elective-policy politics that we're getting now in anticipation of November, 1976.

Graham:

Mayor Bradley, you as a Mayor have had a lot of experience with trying to move Congressmen, and I would like to hear your response as to why the solutions aren't immediate, or are you finding the climate more receptive? What are the problems and the outlook?

Bradley:

Part of the frustration lies in the fact that the Congressmen are now spending so much of their time in Washington that they don't really understand the nature of the problems back home. We try to communicate with them on matters and find that they simply have no understanding of the problems that we face at the city level. We're grateful when we have someone who has had city experience, municipal experience, who rises up the ladder and finds his way back here to Washington. He has a fundamental understanding of some of those problems.

That is in part the nature of this difficulty that we're facing. And then we've got all kinds of lobbying efforts that go on. They're pushed and tugged from every direction by so many interest groups, while we in the city simply don't have the money to hire the lobbyists to be back here to fight those fights for us.

Finally, even if they understood all of our problems and were able to withstand all of the lobbying efforts that they face, they pass the legislation and the President vetoes it.

V

FOREIGN POLICY ISSUES AND THE POLITICAL CAMPAIGN

Here four leading members of Congress—two Democrats and two Republicans—plus a former member, now an independent, address themselves to the foreign policy issues they feel will be debated in the 1976 Presidential campaign and those they feel should be debated but won't. In the process, they advocate a number of solutions of their own.

Senator Mike Mansfield and Representatives John B. Anderson and Donald M. Fraser doubt that foreign policy will figure significantly in the campaign. To the extent real issues are taken up at all, they feel—especially Mr. Anderson—domestic economic issues will predominate. On the whole, they are inclined to be pessimistic about the campaign as a vehicle for clarifying foreign policy. Senator Howard Baker, on the other hand, comes on as an optimist, feeling that foreign policy issues will be "extraordinarily important" in the campaign and that the campaign will prove to be an instrument through which the "sovereign people" will arrive at the right answers.

All the Congressmen are agreed that there is no real mood for isolation in the country; that many aspects of our foreign policy badly need overhauling; that Congress must be heard in both foreign policy formulation and execution. Senators Mansfield and Baker and Representative Anderson feel that a "harder line" in the United Nations is popular and probably desirable, while Rep-

resentative Fraser cautions both about an anti-U.N. pos-
ture and about too much Congressional interference with
Presidential authority to carry out foreign policy. "Fras-
er's Law," he says, teaches that "where the executive
branch makes a mistake in foreign policy you can usually
find Congress right in there with them, cheering them
on."

Eugene McCarthy, although a presidential candi-
date, carries his independent status to the point of more
or less ignoring campaign issues and concentrates on
"procedures, processes and institutions" as being more
important than substantive decisions. But with a typical
McCarthy touch, he advances some foreign policy ideas
which, however unlikely to arise in the campaign, are
nonetheless bold and provocative.

A Drifting Foreign Policy and a Drifting Economy

Mike Mansfield

Foreign policy will be an issue in the 1976 campaign. Barring the unexpected, however, it will be only *an* issue, not *the* issue. The emphasis in the campaign will be on affairs within the nation. In particular, it will be on the state of the nation's economy. Notwithstanding the effort to talk away our economic difficulties, there has yet to be a recovery from the worst recession in forty years. At best, we have managed only to hold on by fingertips; only a marginal momentum has been generated for recovery. The failure to face up to the nation's economic problems is to be seen in the continued high unemployment and inflation. Deeper consequences are visible in a general public disquiet and disaffection with government. Still deeper, in the bedrock of the nation, are the dangerous fissures of social division.

That is hardly a basis on which to build a national contribution to *Pacem in Terris*. So, I reiterate, the prime issue in the coming election will be a meandering economy. Unless we put a stop to the present drift and begin, also, to look with some coordinated foresight to the looming economic problems which are only a few years away,

Mike Mansfield is U.S. Senator from Montana and Senate Majority Leader.

the international role of this nation for the next decade will be, at most, an indifferent one. Indeed, it could even become negative, insofar as contributing to international peace and stability is concerned.

As for foreign affairs, what is likely to be of major consideration in the next election will be the drain of out-dated policies as a contributing factor in the decline of the economy. Unlike earlier years, when money was spent for activities abroad as though the nation had it to burn, every dollar that now goes into anachronistic policies and the military structure to support them is coming not out of an affluent economy, but out of the hides of the people. It is coming from those millions of Americans without tax havens and with no ways to hedge the inflation. Dated foreign policies are a double burden on an already over-burdened segment of the populace.

Expenditures in the name of foreign policy or de-fense, even valid expenditures, require taxes and contrib-ute to the pressure for inflation. If such expenditures are in excess of *contemporary* needs, they strain the economy unnecessarily and, in the end, do harm to the structure of the nation.

Take for example, the policy of stationing troops in all parts of the globe. Whatever relevance such policies may have had in the immediate post-World War II pe-riod, it does not follow that they are still relevant three decades later. Nor does it mean that the nation's defense will collapse if we alter these deployments, scale them down or even in some cases cut them out entirely. Over half a million soldiers were returned from Vietnam with-out endangering the national security. There are other areas where similar adjustments, far less drastic to be sure, seem to me to be entirely possible and very desirable.

The world changes. We have to change with it. But the wheels of government, regrettably, tend to remain in ruts, especially in regard to national security affairs. The lesson of Vietnam, for example, has yet to be learned. Even now an effort is being made to maintain a military position on the Southeast Asian mainland. The executive branch beseeches the Thai government to permit us to keep at least a shadow of our former presence in that nation. What for? A toehold in Thailand will cost the nation millions of dollars—that much is clear. But into what grand design for national security and peace do we fit a few thousand American servicemen and a scattering of mothballed military bases in Thailand? Similarly, there is great reluctance in the government to recognize that over a period of time, there has to be a reduction of U.S. forces in Korea and in Japan.

The emphasis of policy in Asia, in short, is as it has been for the past quarter of a century or more. It remains an emphasis on the United States as a "military defender." There is, to be sure, a military role for the United States to play in the Western Pacific. In any integrated concept of a durable peace in that region, however, the accent should have long since shifted to multilateral diplomacy and on how to sustain an expansion of commerce and other mutually beneficial relationships. In such a concept, too, I should think that we would have already moved to try to establish regular diplomatic relations with the present governments in Vietnam, Cambodia and Laos as a contribution to stabilizing the situation in Asia.

That course would also be the best way to permit a final resolution of doubts concerning those still missing in action as a result of the Indochina war. It is not a sufficient answer to the question of their fate to proclaim over and over again our national concern or to memorialize our sympathy. Nor is there any real contribution to the peace of mind of the families of those still missing in demanding with words what cannot be obtained in the absence of diplomatic contact. That course, in my judgment, borders on making a political mockery of human heartaches.

It is time to get final answers on the MIA's. It is time to find out what can be found out and then to let the dead rest in peace. It is reprehensible in the extreme to treat the war casualties of this nation as "bargaining chips" of diplomacy or the pawns of politics.

In any design for durable peace, it is also time to drop the approach which led us into the misadventure in Indochina and into two decades of alienation as regards the people of China. It is time to discard the assumption that this nation's power is such as to be able to control the flow of events on the Asian mainland. Vietnam should have made clear that our ability even to exercise a rational influence on the affairs of that continent is limited. Underscoring the point are the wasted years and the squandered resources in dealing with China on the basis of the long-distance hostility of cold war.

The United States is, in my judgment, not an Asian power but a major Pacific nation. The difference is more than semantic. It is the difference between a sensible acceptance of the realities of Asia and the dangerous illusions of military omnipotence. It is the difference between what this nation can reasonably do for peace and freedom and the serious damage which it does to itself when it presumes to do more.

The outer limits of our unilateral and bilateral defense in the Pacific, in my judgment, are the Aleutians, Japan and the Philippines. Beyond that, insofar as this nation is concerned, the enhancement of the nation's security is properly sought in developing multilateral relationships of peace and in strengthening bilateral relationships with Asian governments, preferably those strongly rooted in their own people. In short, the projections of the military defense of the Western approaches to the United States should be confined to the Pacific Ocean. We ought not, as we have done, presume to extend them on to the Asian mainland.

Nor, in the name of defense, should we pursue a course which leads us militarily into a third ocean, the Indian Ocean, and its adjacent lands. The first step in that direction, I regret to say, has been taken by the back-door acquisition of Diego Garcia through questionable leasing practices. The development of that base is probably the opening gun in a campaign to build an Indian Ocean fleet. What for? What interests of the people of this nation are involved that they should be called on to pay for a third-ocean navy? In truth, we have neither the manpower nor the resources to engage in an arms buildup in the Indian Ocean, without massive increases in Federal expenditures. If the Diego Garcia boondoggle materializes, what we will have gained, in my judgment, is not greater security for this nation but a further weakening of our capacity to meet the real needs of the American people. We will have established the nucleus of another massive burden of taxes and inflation.

One hopeful sign in this situation is that the Senate on its own responsibility and the House in conference with the Senate, directed that appropriations for fiscal 1976, except for a $250,000 safeguard—on the airfield at Diego Garcia—be held off until April 1. During that period, the President has been asked to try to negotiate a settlement with the Soviet Union which could preclude both powers from establishing bases in the Indian Ocean. That is not much because if we are determined to waste our substance, I expect that the Russians are not going to help us to save it. At least, however, the measure does permit a brief period to stop, look and listen before we proceed further along this course.

On the other side of the globe, we have in excess of 500,000 military personnel and dependents in Western Europe, thirty years after the end of the Second World War. It is probably the most costly single expenditure for a nonproductive purpose in the Federal budget. This anachronistic deployment is a relic of World War II and the early years of the Cold War. Whatever relevance it may have once had to the nation's security has all but disappeared. Even as an interim measure, the U.S. military deployment in Europe has little significance in its present form, to the search for a durable peace in Europe. Much less does it relate to the actual defense of that continent

against an invasion from the East. Nevertheless, the drain
on U.S. military manpower and U.S. dollars is unabated.
I can only reiterate what I have said many times over the
past dozen years or more: The deployment can and should
be cut substantially and unilaterally in line with the interests of the United States. It will not weaken our defense,
in my judgment; rather, it will strengthen the nation by
lightening the burden on the economy.

As of last July, including this European deployment,
we had a total of 518,000 military personnel overseas. In
addition, 37,000 U.S. citizens and in the neighborhood of
150,000 foreign nationals were engaged as civilian employees in support of these forces. Finally, 370,000 dependents of U.S. servicemen were overseas to accompany
them. The total is 1,060,000 people, in one form or another stationed abroad, paid for by U.S. taxpayers, for what
are termed "defense purposes." Not even mentioned are
bargain-basement sales or gifts of military equipment to
other nations also, presumably, for U.S. defense or foreign policy purposes. The subsidized cost of these activities, too, is borne by the people of the nation.

If, as the executive branch contends, the role of world
policeman for this nation has been rejected, then where is
the pattern in this vast military commitment abroad? The
fact is that there is no pattern. What this nation has
abroad, supports abroad and promotes abroad, is a com-
posite put together out of carry-overs of World War II,
the Korean War and the Southeast Asian misadventure.
Add to this motley collection, a host of random undertakings over a period of several decades often for purposes
long since forgotten. Add to it, finally, military aid to
dozens of countries and vigorous arms merchandising by
the Defense Department in the manner of some latter-day
Sir Basil Zaharoff.

Who is trying to sort out this immense, disparate and
costly conglomerate? Where is the effort being made to
separate the wheat from the chaff? The wasteful from the
necessary? Where are the up-to-date integrated strategic

concepts into which to fit specific U.S. defense activities abroad? The answers to these questions have yet to be supplied. They must be forthcoming. They are, in my judgment, an absolute requisite both for the restoration of the U.S. economy and for an effective U.S. contribution to peace on earth in the years ahead.

Foreign Policy and
the Price of Hogs in Chicago

John B. Anderson

We are here to explore what we consider to be the "key foreign policy issues in the 1976 campaign." This topic permits us all on the panel to engage in one of our favorite political pastimes—crystal ball gazing. I do think it's important though that everyone understand the ground rules for this sport: we cannot be called back a year from now, after the 1976 elections, and be held accountable for our predictions.

Allow me to come right out front at the outset with my own prejudices about foreign policy and presidential campaigns—prejudices, I might add, which are based on my own fifteen-year experience in national politics. I first ran for Congress in 1960—the same year, of course, in which Mr. Nixon narrowly lost the presidency to Senator Kennedy. In considering today's topic, I am reminded of some advice given to Vice President Nixon by our Illinois Governor Bill Stratton, at the Republican convention that summer, and I quote: "You can say all you want about foreign affairs, but what is really important is the price of

John B. Anderson is a member of the U.S. House of Representatives and Chairman of the House Republican Conference.

hogs in Chicago and St. Louis." Stephen Hess, writing on
this subject in the Fall, 1972, issue of *Foreign Policy*
magazine, notes that it was ironic for Nixon that foreign
policy was not a dominant issue in the 1960 campaign—remember Quemoy and Matsu?—since it has
played a dominant role in every election since 1960. Hess
goes on to make the following four observations about
foreign policy and Presidential campaigns, with which I
happen to agree:

> We have not witnessed serious, responsible debate on foreign
> policy during the presidential campaigns;
>
> The American voter is not particularly knowledgeable about
> foreign policy issues;
>
> The electorate's interest in foreign policy does not go much
> beyond a basic yearning for peace; and finally
>
> Foreign policy issues have not necessarily been decisive, even
> though they were dominant.

If you briefly review the Presidential elections since
1960, I think you will concur in the validity of these observations:

> In 1964, President Johnson benefited from the public's hawkish
> perception of Senator Goldwater—remember the little girl
> plucking a daisy juxtaposed with the nuclear countdown and ex-
> plosion ad?
>
> In 1968, the American people were ready for a change in our
> Vietnam policy, and that meant to them a change in parties;
>
> And in 1972, our Vietnam policy had changed, albeit slowly, and
> President Nixon was exploring new avenues of detente with
> China and the Soviet Union.

But in each of these campaigns, foreign policy issues
were not actively, thoroughly, and responsibly debated,
nor were they decisive. At the same time, the very basic
yearning for peace played a dominant role in those elections. What I am saying then, mostly on the basis of past
experience, is that foreign policy issues are not likely to be
a central focus of the 1976 campaign, but will still play a

dominant role, though subliminal in nature, to the extent that the electorate perceives that a particular candidate has done or will do more to advance the interests of peace.

I am inclined to agree with an observation made some years ago by our present U.N. Ambassador, Daniel Patrick Moynihan, that elections are rarely our finest hour since issues have a way of being oversimplified, over-dramatized, and overcatastrophized. Moynihan goes on to caution against expectations that campaigns are or will be appropriate vehicles for objective, thorough and balanced reviews of public policy. While this rule applies equally to domestic and foreign policy, and, as Stephen Hess has pointed out, while all issues are handled badly "foreign policy issues are handled worst."

I would be delighted if I could be proved wrong in 1976, but I don't think it is likely. This convocation has dealt with what I consider to be the major issues which should be seriously and responsibly addressed by candidates of both parties in 1976: detente, the impact of foreign policy on our domestic economy, international economic policy, American defense policy and our foreign commitments, the role of the United Nations and our role in it, and the role of our foreign intelligence apparatus and its impact and relevance to the democratic process.

These are all very legitimate and vital foreign policy concerns, and ideally they should be thoroughly considered and debated in a presidential campaign. I feel this to be especially necessary in what I consider to be a crucial period of transition for the United States, when we are groping for a post-Vietnam and post-Watergate identity for our nation. Like most members of Congress, I am acutely aware of public frustration, uncertainty and declining confidence in government which has resulted from these traumas of our recent past, and present. And yet, when I consider how incapable we are, even in the Congress—what we fondly refer to as the world's greatest deliberative body—to debate seriously and to resolve these problems, I am even less sanguine that they can somehow receive the serious attention that they deserve in the heat of a presidential campaign.

Let me give you just one example. The first item which I mentioned that should be a central focus of our national foreign policy debate is detente. It seems that we have fallen from our euphoric high over detente in 1972, when President Nixon opened new doors with China and the Soviet Union, to a state in which the public is somewhat disillusioned and even a little fearful about what this policy means. The pollsters tell us that the public still favors pursuing a policy of detente with our adversaries, but that it feels we should be getting more out of it than we are. In brief, there is a perception, given the results of the first major wheat deal with the Soviets and reports that they may be gaining a strategic edge over us, that we have been taken for suckers, or have been given the short end of the stick. My own assessment is that this new mood is a consequence of excessive expectations at the outset about what detente was or could produce.

There is a considerable difference between detente as a relaxation of tensions, and detente as the millennium. And I think the public's initial interpretation of detente mistakenly inclined toward the latter. The new mood, to my mind, is both justified and realistic. Nevertheless, all this is most worthy of a national debate over just where we are today in our relations with the Soviets and Chinese, where we're going with detente and what we expect out of it.

But consider, if you will, the contradictory pronouncements about detente made by a major Democratic presidential contender in just three days of campaigning, as reported by the *Washington Star*. In quiet press conferences, the candidate was willing to say: "I'm not against detente," but only concerned that it be an even and realistic exchange between the United States and the Soviet Union. Before a nonpartisan audience in my state of Illinois, he elaborated: "It had better be a two-way rather than a one-way street. It can't be all give and no take." But then, moving on to Florida, he said: "I'm not for this phony detente where we do all the giving and they do all the taking." And that same night, in another Florida city, and before a receptive audience, he said the following: "Detente? That's a highfalutin term to cover up a lot of skullduggery."

If this is an example of the type of foreign policy debate we're going to have in 1976, and I suspect it is—and from all candidates—than I don't think 1976 is going to be anymore a highwater mark for serious foreign policy discussions than past campaigns have been.

In conclusion, barring any major international incidents, and I don't for a moment count those out, I frankly don't see foreign policy issues as being highly marketable products in the 1976 campaign; the public demand is just not there. To the extent that they are marketed by candidates as a sideline, they will not be quality products; quality workmanship is just not one of the strong points of our campaign factories. To the extent that foreign policy issues are marketed, they will be negligible in terms of their educational redeeming value; campaigns are designed to enliven rather than to enlighten.

For those of us who are interested and knowledgeable about such issues, simply because it's part of our vocation or avocation, we can rightfully ask: why can't a campaign be more like this convocation?—just as Rex Harrison in "My Fair Lady" asked, "why can't a woman, be more like a man?" I think both parties would ideally like to elevate campaigns to such a level of serious, rational and responsible debate over domestic and foreign policy issues. The series of Democratic Policy Conferences are one example of this desire.

But in all candor, in the final analysis, you have to recognize that such debates and conferences and convocations tend to attract the same people: the hardcore party faithful, the ideologues, the intellectuals and the causers. As much as I favor structural and substantive reforms of our parties and political process, I don't think any amount of tinkering is going to make serious public policy consumers out of the electorate. The general issues of peace and the pocketbook will continue to dominate our campaigns, and, as recent elections have shown, decisions at the ballot box will more often be made on the basis of whom or what we're against than whom or what we are for.

By this critique, I by no means wish to imply that political leaders should abandon any hope of or responsibility for educating the public on important foreign policy issues. But I would suggest that there is very little hope or possibility of using political campaigns as the proper device for accomplishing this objective. I realize that in this brief statement I have not dealt substantively with any of the foreign policy challenges confronting our nation today. I purposely avoided doing so here because I think most candidates will avoid doing so in their campaigns in 1976. In short, I reject the implication in the title of our panel that there will be *"key* foreign policy issues in the 1976 campaign."

What the People Want
and What They Don't Want

Howard H. Baker, Jr.

I believe that the 1976 campaigns are destined to be extraordinarily important to the development of fundamental policy to serve this country as we begin the third century of our existence.

I suppose most politicians have at one time or another declared that their particular generation is faced with the most difficult and complex problems ever presented to civilization; and many of them clearly have been right. No generation, however, has ever had a clearer claim to that distress than we do. It is true that other governments and people have faced difficult times indeed, including our own War of Independence, the War Between the States, and the two World Wars. But there is a distinguishing difference between now and then, and that difference is the undoubted ability of mankind to incinerate itself in a nuclear holocaust.

So, from the moment of the first nuclear explosion in New Mexico in 1945, the relevance and importance of foreign policy and national defense were permanently

Howard H. Baker, Jr. is U.S. Senator from Tennessee and Co-Chairman of the Senate Select Committee on Campaign Practices.

established as the paramount concerns of this nation.

The ultimate question of survival as a nation-state in a hostile world is further complicated by those other recently delivered blessings of science and technology—instantaneous electronic communications and, almost instantaneous transportation of both warheads and people. And we are faced with the prospect not only of defending ourselves against the threat of other nuclear powers, but containing or diminishing the disruptions that occur inevitably as the have-nots of the world find out how much the haves really have.

It is against this backdrop that I view the importance of the American political system. For I think it is clear that none of us participating in this convocation can honestly lay claim to definitive solutions for the spectrum of dilemma which now confronts and will shortly confront mankind. But I am reassured by the observation that, by and large, in the course of the past two hundred years the American people themselves, acting together in their collective genius and sovereign capacity, have been remarkably right in most of their decisions; and I suspect that they will be right as they confront the future.

It is the political system and the campaign of 1976, and the others of the past and those of the future, which serve as the vehicle by which the sovereign expresses the range of its demands and dissent.

It is axiomatic that politicians and bureaucrats must work feverishly to keep up with the public, and I think that this time in our national existence is no exception. I think in international affairs that the sovereign is far ahead of the government in its evolution and development of the country's first new foreign policy since, at least, World War II.

Even before our disengagement from Vietnam, it should have been clear that we were revising if not in fact discarding the principle which had served us well for a very long time indeed; that is to say that the protection of this country from distant harm should depend both on the

ocean moat surrounding us and a system of alliances—
most recently through the Asian Crescent and behind the
shield of NATO.

I am frank to say that I do not know what our new
foreign policy will be. The sovereign has not yet fully
disclosed what it will be. Of course, that is the problem of
having a plural sovereign of 200 million people.
Sometimes the intent is difficult to perceive clearly or it is
made clear only after the event in question.

I do have some ideas, however, about what the
sovereign will dictate that it shall not be.

I do not believe America will retreat into a classic
isolationism. I think that both impractical and un-
desirable. On the other hand, I do not believe that we are
likely in the foreseeable future to commit our troop
strength or substantial military force to direct involvement in other Vietnams without the most serious
national debate and careful coordination between the
Congress and the White House.

Korea might be the single exception. I believe
America's commitment to defense of South Korea
against the potential aggression from the North is such
that the government and the country would fully support retaliation against a North Korean invasion.

I do not think the United States will abandon our experiment in detente. I believe that this effort initiated by
former President Nixon will be recognized in the future as
a courageous, and I hope, successful redeeming grace of
his troubled Administration. I believe there are dangers in
detente; but I believe there are greater dangers in return-
ing to the canons of the Cold War. So, I suspect that the
campaign of 1976 will indicate that the sovereign ap-
proves of our efforts to reestablish a dialogue with our
recent and erstwhile adversaries, and to elaborate and expand our trade opportunities with them.

In this vein, I believe we will not ignore the moral and
pragmatic imperative of continuing to assist the
developing world in its efforts to improve the human con-

dition. It must be, and I believe it will be, recognized that this nation has a vested and vital interest in the elimination of poverty and hunger throughout the world community.

I do not think that the functional structure of government for the formulation and execution of foreign policy will be substantially changed, for I think the sovereign has a good appreciation of how well it has served in the past and how relevant it is to the future. Specifically, I think we will not see the Congress substantially diminish the inherent authority of the President as Chief Magistrate to execute foreign policy. But, I think, there is heightened importance attaching to the constitutional role of the Congress, and particularly the Senate, in the formulation of general foreign policy principles. I believe that the soverign is telling us to establish a workable partnership and not the domination of one over the other.

And finally, I suspect that in this and subsequent elections, the country, the sovereign, will turn its attention increasingly to the problem of the proliferation of nuclear weapons.

The nuclear club has grown from a single member to seven nations which either have or could quickly assemble an explosive nuclear device. There are probably twelve other countries fully capable of doing so at this time. And, even more alarming, there are probably fifty corporations or private industrial groups in the world who have the resources, technology, and talent to create a nuclear capability as non-national entities. I suspect that the containment of the nuclear threat may be the ultimate foreign policy problem.

In this complex society, it is not possible effectively to separate foreign policy from domestic considerations in many fields, and certainly not in the field of nuclear power. I believe, for example, that it is necessary for us to depend on nuclear power for our energy requirements in the foreseeable future. But, in doing so, we must be acutely aware of the fact that we are extending the risk of a proliferation of nuclear capability to other nations and even to non-national organizations and increasing the danger of the loss or theft of nuclear weapons or materials, particularly in view of the increasing terrorist activity.

And so, while I have no definitive answers for the major problems that confront the United States in the field of foreign policy, and while I perceive grave threats to the continuation of the existence of mankind, as well as peaceful nation states, in this nuclear era, I am essentially not pessimistic. For I have an extraordinary faith in that collective genius of the American people and in the machinery of the political system they have chosen as their means of expressing their judgment. I believe that just as we, as a nation, have been remarkably right on most of the major decisions in the past, we will be right again in the future. And I believe that we are uniquely equipped—by virtue of our structure and form of government, the heightened social consciousness of the American people, a growing awareness of our non-insular existence and our knowledge of our responsibilities for the future—to give leadership to the rest of the world in our quest for survival.

Foreign Policy and the Lack of Consensus

Donald M. Fraser

I am grateful for this opportunity to speak here because this *Pacem in Terris* Convocation may be one of the few times in which these issues will be thoughtfully explored.

I share with Senator Mansfield the view that the American public's attention in 1976 will be centered on the economic difficulties facing the United States. And that does have implications for international policy. Because it is in times of high unemployment that we find that the opposition to expanded or liberalized trade increases, a time when opposition to economic assistance to other countries grows. This is evidenced, for example, by the recent conference of Democratic mayors, in which they outlined a program for the United States Congress. In the beginning of their program they called for a cut not only in military assistance—a view which I share with them—but also a reduction in economic assistance to the poorer countries of the world. So unless we do solve our economic distress here at home it will be significantly

Donald M. Fraser is a member of the U.S. House of Representatives and a member of the United States Delegation to the United Nations.

more difficult to conduct a wise foreign policy in behalf of the United States.

As we approach 1976, we begin with less consensus in America than we've had for a long time. There's no consensus on the nature of the threat that faces us; there is, therefore, no consensus on the kind of force and force structure we need in the military services. There's no consensus as to whether we really need to continue this elaborate, far-flung system of treaties involving us with some forty-five nations around the world; there is no consensus, as Senator Mansfield has demonstrated, on the importance of maintaining 300,000 troops in Europe. And clearly there's no consensus on whether we should maintain programs of military and economic aid abroad.

There will be some issues that I think will inject themselves in the campaign which it might be just as well if they didn't. For example, there may well be a continuing debate about whether the Soviet Union has violated the spirit, if not the letter, of the SALT agreement. I would regard this as an unfortunate element to try to settle in a national campaign or debate in a presidential year. It is a matter that the congressional committees ought to look into with some care and resolve, so that it doesn't become an ongoing element in which bias and ignorance predominate.

Second, there is likely to be continuing debate, and it was already heard in earlier sessions of the convocation, about the significance of the present size of the Soviet armed forces and the question of where they are going. This argument will center not only on the military consequences but even more importantly on the political consequences. In some respects, we are in trouble on this because the Pentagon has lost its credibility as an informer of the American public about these matters. We have watched too often the Pentagon come to the Congress, around the time of appropriations, and issue its new set of warnings about the sudden surge in Soviet strength. The Pentagon, for example, has managed to discover a strategic bomber about to be born in the Soviet arsenal once every year over the last decade.

Third, there is likely to be the issue of the Panama Canal, which is a legitimate issue, but one I rather regret may be injected into the 1976 campaign because it is so susceptible of demagoguery. This reflects my view, of course, which is that the United States must take a rather enlightened approach to the need to disengage from a more or less total control of that piece of land that divides Panama.

Let me turn to some issues that at least some of us feel strongly about. First, for me, is to elevate in American foreign policy our concerns about human rights. I argue for this not only because it would help to redeem an important element of American foreign policy in relation to our basic value system, but I would suggest that an increased sensitivity to the violations of human rights of a gross and sustained nature are often an early warning indicator of trouble in the world. Not every set of gross violations of human rights will evoke civil conflict, or conflict between countries, but where there is conflict, where there is civil war, very often it is the abuse of human rights which lies at the foundation of it.

We sit here today, having been signatories to the Helsinki agreement, with its Third Basket emphasis on human rights, and watch the Soviet Union deny Sakharov the right to go to collect the Nobel Prize. Is this a matter where we simply say, well, that's just the way it is? Or do we say that the Helsinki agreement ought to have some meaning in the Third Basket, which was an interest very strongly pushed by the United States and Western Europe? And, further, should United States forces underwrite an experiment in rather absolute political repression by the government of South Korea? In my judgment, if they want to experiment with that kind of government, so be it, but not with the United States forces underwriting it.

We clearly need to keep the momentum of the U.N.

Seventh Special Session on economic cooperation, the need to move forward vigorously and quickly to an international system of food reserves, finding ways to protect primary commodity exporters in the very violent fluctuations of their earnings. We need to keep our intentions clear about our commitment to building international institutions.

The Zionist resolution was one of the sharpest setbacks to those of us who support the U.N. that has been experienced in many years. There is a marked tendency to want to retaliate against the institution itself, as though the United Nations, which hires the General Assembly hall and provides the seats, also casts the votes. The votes came from those countries which, for one reason or another, felt that this was a proper resolution to adopt. If we feel enough about it, and I feel strongly about it, this is a matter that ought to be taken up in bilateral channels with those countries, not against the institution which simply provided the meeting hall.

But whether or not the Zionist resolution is a cause of lessened support for the United Nations, we must keep building the institutions that surround the whole U.N. family. And the new efforts in food and population and environment and law of the seas bear witness to the importance of a positive posture in support of these institutions.

The reshaping of our military posture is another important issue. We clearly should moderate the growth of the strategic weapons. We can't stop our research and development, but we ought to slow it down. We need to take the opportunity to see if moderation may not in fact prove to be as useful as SALT agreements. This is one area which, unchecked, creates its own instability and its own threats to the world.

And we clearly need a more realistic assessment of the threats of a conventional nature to the United States in order to shape our conventional forces accordingly. If we are to do that, we could save money, and then we could increase the amount of economic resources that we make available to the Third World. We stand at the bottom of the Western nations in our economic transfers. Our present percentage is about one-quarter of one percent. Western Europe, on the average, is double that amount.

Finally, there is a need for a new consensus which may flow from the fact of the 1976 election itself. I hope this comes, because, even as I participate in it, I fear the growing intrusion of Congress into the foreign affairs field. I say that as one of the authors of the War Powers Act. But I have what I call Fraser's law. And that is that where the executive branch makes a mistake in foreign policy, you can usually find Congress right in there with them, cheering them on. But where only one makes a mistake, I am afraid the history of our country suggests that it has more often been the Congress itself.

What we need to do is to find our way to the broader consensus about where American interests lie, what our responsibilities are, and then work with the executive branch in a constructive way, but of course always subjecting that executive branch to rather careful scrutiny. I'm hopeful. I think we're on our way toward that result, but we'll know more after November, 1976.

The Need for
New Approaches

Eugene J. McCarthy

Senator Mansfield should have taken more credit for himself. He was one of the first persons to speak out against our involvement in Vietnam. Earlier than that, in the midfifties, he in the Senate and some of us in the House said that something should be done about the Central Intelligence Agency. Not because we necessarily knew what it was doing, but because we sensed that it was an institutional contradiction of American democracy. This leads me to the point I want to emphasize here, which concerns procedures and processes and institutions more than substantive decisions.

The American Constitution gives only a few lines to purposes and nothing to substantive proposals, but it goes on for page after page dealing with the question of how you make democracy work in domestic government. I think we ought to be more concerned about methods and forms of action in the base from which we operate if we try to deal with foreign policy, if we expect it to be particularly successful.

Eugene J. McCarthy is a former U.S. Senator from Minnesota.

It was as though it was a revelation when Marshall McLuhan said the "medium is the message." Actually the men who drafted the Constitution of this country understood the same thing, and in fact they almost said that the procedure and the process, the constitutional methodology, is the message of democracy. We have forgotten that, to some extent at home but even more in foreign policy—neglecting to consider the condition in the context out of which policy is made and giving too little thought to the method by which we attempt to enforce it and to the means by which we attempt to involve other people in the determination of that policy. As I see it, we have a problem of undoing a number of misconceptions that have developed over a period of roughly twenty years, I suppose, since the end of World War II.

In the years immediately after 1945, we began to do two things. We began a process of demilitarization. The defense budgets under Harry Truman before Korea got down to about $15 or $16 billion a year. We had put our trust largely in the United Nations as the instrumentality through which we thought future foreign policy might be determined, or at least to some extent agreed to. And we said we will emphasize not military action, but we will use our economic power to try to do some good and give some direction to the way in which the world may move. That attitude and those commitments lasted only a short time. We had the interruption of the Korean war. After that we never retreated or backed away from militarization.

President Eisenhower, in his last year, had a defense budget of something like $45 billion, which was six years after the war had ended, and it was rather nice of him, in his farewell address, to warn us about the military-industrial complex. What he should have said was, "Look, I let it develop, and I've left it there for you. It happened during my Administration." And, in fact, that was when it was established. So we got into a process of militarization from which we never really have backed away.

I don't mean to leave the burden with the Republicans and Eisenhower, because the campaign of 1960 was based largely upon what was said to be a "missile gap." It turned out that there wasn't one. But in any case it opened up a whole new area of military competition. And then added to that, of course, was Cuba and subsequent to that almost an unlimited increase in nuclear expansion.

On the other hand we began to back away from the use of international agencies. It was rather subtle, under John Foster Dulles, who was the greatest Covenanter since John Calvin. He began to organize separate agreements—SEATO, etc. Well, what did that do to the U.N.? They said it was regionalism. If you have regionalism, then you don't have the United Nations. Dulles had every continent organized as a separate region as far as he could, excepting Africa, and he was working on that. It was a subtle attack upon the idea of a world organization in which you would try to work out international differences, a subtle retreat.

I suppose the high point of that withdrawal was manifested when President Nixon addressed the United Nations. And he challenged them in five or six areas. He said they really ought to do something about peace keeping. That was at a time when he was conducting the war in Vietnam. He said they ought to do something about drug traffic, when we were creating the demand for most of the international drug traffic. He said they ought to do something about the have and have-not nations. I think that year we were arguing about an economic aid program of a billion three hundred million dollars, which is a really significant contribution out of a gross national product of something over a trillion dollars. He said they ought to concern themselves with the pollution of the ocean. That was, I think, two weeks after we dropped nerve gas off the coast of Florida. And he said they ought to do something about the pollution of the atmosphere of the earth. We were defoliating in Vietnam, and we were the worst polluters in the history of the world.

In our retreat from reliance on international organization, the question of substance was, of course, important, but the questions of procedure and method, the context in which you operate, was more so. I would like to suggest we rethink and revise our approach in three major areas.

First, with reference to demilitarization, we really ought to act unilaterally just to change the context out of which we attempt to talk about disarmament. Some mention was made of nuclear proliferation. Now seven nations can produce nuclear weapons. There are twenty corporations in this country that can do it. And proliferation is a matter not of nations but of the number of bombs. And the nations that have proliferated most are the United States and Russia. If I were a nation that had signed a non-proliferation treaty, I would be upset.

If the Americans and the Russians were in perfect balance so they couldn't waste a bomb, everybody might feel at ease. But they've got excess capacity now. They don't have to worry about each other. They could bomb a few other nations and still not be short in terms of what they need for each other. Yet we applaud the Secretary of State who goes to SALT talks and says he is going to cap the race at a point where they will have enough to do us in twenty times, and we will have enough to do them in twenty times. And then we use words like parity, or equivalence. We could move ourselves to put a limit upon what we're going to manufacture in the way of nuclear weapons without endangering our security in any way.

Secondly, we could also move in the area of conventional weapons. The whole question of conventional weapons now doesn't have much meaning in terms of warfare, but it relates to the entire military-industrial complex whereby you produce new conventional weapons which are superior to the ones that were used in the last war. We could win World War II now in about three weeks if we fought it again. We have better airplanes now, better tanks, better transport. But what does it come to? We produce a superior jet plane, and then we can sell the old ones. You have to get rid of obsolete airplanes and other mistakes of the Pentagon. You can't leave them on the runways. And this in effect is what they were doing.

Now, you could turn it around and say, look, the military have to have something to do. They can't spend all their time jogging back and forth over Memorial Bridge. It's not a good public image. And there is something to be said for having them occupied so they don't have contingency plans for wars. You could bring back the cavalry. There is no reason why, when you're dealing with conventional warfare, it has to be an upward movement. You could move backward and say, look, we've decided the F-17 is operationally too efficient, so we are now going to produce an older-type airplane, and finally work it down to cavalry.

What you have to do is to change procedure so you don't have the pressures which allow people to be irrational. Now the pressure is for getting rid of the obsolete and for developing new things for the military. It is a process which in effect forces military arms sales. This leads to the establishment of military aid missions, and thus the whole array of what we call the military-industrial complex is maintained, not by a particular design from outside, but because we have paid too little attention to methodology and to the context within which people act.

Thirdly, I think we should abolish the Special Forces and really restore the Marines to their traditional position. With the Marines, you always knew when they landed, and you always knew when they disembarked. With the Special Forces you don't know when they go in, you don't know when they leave, you don't know what they do while they're there, and you're not sure that they've gone.

In the area of procedure in international diplomacy, I also think we ought to reexamine all of these regional arrangements we have, SEATO, CENTO, even the OAS, to see whether or not we want to cancel them out and move back again into the United Nations. And we ought to repeal all the triggering resolutions we've adopted, like the Middle East Resolution, which said in effect that if a government invites you in because it's threatened by communism, the President can respond. Under that guise we went into Lebanon and were prepared to go into Cuba. The plan was to establish a beachhead and then to have them say, "We are the government, and we're threatened by communism." In the case of the Dominican Republic, we found that the first message that came in was that a military junta was taking over, and the Administration said, "Send us another message which says it's communistic, and then we can respond." And then they did send another message. And we did respond.

Finally, we ought to put limitations upon the Central Intelligence Agency so it is not a kind of separate operating foreign policy agency. If things have to be done, they ought to be done in the normal diplomatic ways of the State Department and by traditional international and justifiable foreign policy standards. And we ought to begin to use constructively our economic power, the power of food and fiber, of technology and of money.

If we can put all of these things back together—a limited military commitment, a fuller use of our economic capacity, and a new emphasis upon the integrity of the ideals of America—then I think the substance of what we decide to do will almost take care of itself because the process and the procedure and the tradition will so set the direction, the pattern, that we will not have to be apologetic in 1984.

VI

BIPARTISAN FOREIGN POLICY AND THE MALAISE OF GOVERNMENT

*With Harry Ashmore, Edward Morgan and Audrey Top-
ping joining the Congressmen and Eugene McCarthy,
there is a lively exchange about bipartisan foreign policy,
American attitudes toward the United Nations, the difficulties of detente and whether there is a "gap" between
the people and the government. The consensus is that
bipartisanship in foreign policy is bad and that attitudes
toward the U.N. have hardened. There is general if vague
agreement that some kind of detente is necessary and
desirable, but all except Senator McCarthy feel it is in for
a rough time politically. There is expressed a strong feeling that if there is not a gap between people and government there is at least a woeful lack of confidence in public
institutions and politicians. Senator Baker sees the two-
party system as temporarily in disarray but believes it is
about to be reinvigorated. Additional items taken up are
utilization of nuclear weapons stockpiles for peacetime
energy uses and the dangers of nuclear proliferation.*

Harry S. Ashmore:

The basic question is whether we do have, or ever did have, or should have, a bipartisan foreign policy. This has been a slogan we have lived by in this country since World War II, the concept of an agreed-upon approach to foreign affairs by the leaders of the Republican and Democratic parties. It emerged in the Roosevelt Administration, carried over to the Truman Administration, and held up reasonably well through the Korean war. It finally broke down in the course of the Vietnamese war. I would like to ask Senator Mansfield his general view of the congressional obligation to maintain a bipartisan foreign policy.

Mansfield:

I do not think bipartisan foreign policy is a good thing. I don't think the Congress ought to agree with everything the President does, or by the same token the President with the Congress. I think we should have a certain degree

---

Harry S. Ashmore is an Associate of the Center for the Study of Democratic Institutions and former Editor-in-Chief of the Encyclopaedia Britannica.

of independence, and we ought to understand one another. Instead of using the old Vandenberg phrase that partisan politics stops at the water's edge, we ought to have more consultation at the takeoff between the President and at least the leadership and the appropriate members of the appropriate committees in the Congress.

Too often, the President, the Secretary of State, the Secretary of Defense, and the National Security Council make policy without congressional consultation. One of the weaknesses of Presidents in recent years, especially those who have served in the Congress, is that they forget their old friends down there in whom they can confide and whom they can trust. The Presidents have become more and more isolated in the White House, and those people who are not elected—the Secretary of State, the Secretary of Defense, the head of the N.S.C., those anonymous assistants and some not so anonymous—are the ones who have the greatest effect.

Maybe in wartime a bipartisan foreign policy is good because you've got no choice. But outside of that, I think that neither we nor the Executive should lose our independence, but that we should consult together and try to arrive at a reasonable and a functioning kind of foreign policy.

Baker:

I don't really think there is much difference in point of view on the Republican side about how we ought to approach foreign policy, in terms of the political divisions in the country. I think there is nothing special about foreign policy or defense policy that sets it apart from or above the political process. I think it's essential that the political system take account of evolving and developing new concerns and factors and take account of the construction of new foreign policy.

I think the wartime bipartisan foreign policy of the Vandenberg type is the product of a natural evolution and development. That is, a great national threat is more than a philosophy or a choice or a method of operations. I can see times in the future, times when you very well might have another bipartisan foreign policy. You might indeed, have another coalition Cabinet with the President appointing a Secretary of State or Secretary of Defense from the opposition party. But more likely than not that would be the result of a great external threat, not a result of the functioning of the political system.

The salient single point to remember is there is nothing sacrosanct about foreign policy or defense policy that sets it apart from the ordinary conflict of partisan political debate.

Ashmore:

Senator McCarthy, as I understand it, you have been ranging somewhere outside the limits, the ordained limits at least, of the conventional political parties. You have sounded on occasion as though you were leaning toward the creation of a third or a fourth party. How does it look out there to you? Do you see a revival of partisan politics on foreign policy, or a departure from it?

McCarthy:

Well, I don't mind a revival of partisan politics as long as it isn't Republican and Democratic.

Of course, we have had bipartisan foreign policy. There hasn't been any partisan dispute. Vietnam was a bipartisan war. There were only half a dozen members of the Senate who opposed the war in Vietnam, one or two Republicans, four or five Democrats. It was a bipartisan war. The militarization of American foreign policy in the years after 1952 was bipartisan. It was just a question of rivalry as to who could militarize it the most.

The ideology was provided pretty much by the Republicans, but the military hardware was provided by the

Democrats. Dulles gave us the ideology but the Democrats came on with Robert McNamara, who said we must be prepared for two and one-half wars. It was not a question of Democrats against Republicans.

Actually the arms race has not been between the United States and the Soviet Union. It has been between each succeeding Administration and the previous one. If we could only stop that arms race we would be in pretty good shape.

In the Eisenhower campaign, they said we were underdefended by Truman, so they raised the ante to 46 billion dollars. Kennedy said we were underdefended by Eisenhower, so they got the budget up to about 65 or 70 billion. Johnson said we were underdefended, Nixon said we were underdefended. Gerald Ford said the other day that we were now the strongest we had ever been, and when Mr. Rumsfeld was sworn in he said we were ready to take on everybody. We ought to inaugurate a President sometime who doesn't first bring God in and then declare war on the rest of the world. This has been the race, a bipartisan competition to see who could have more defense. And the foreign policy has reflected that.

We get into artificial controversies which John Adams warned us against. He said the worst thing you could have in this republic is to have politics divided between two strong factions. He said it's a prescription for irresponsibility.

I think this is clearly manifest in two ways. One, you have excessive party loyalty. Democrats showed it in supporting Johnson and the war in Vietnam. Then they turned against the war after the same war was being conducted by Nixon, in the same way. The Republicans, most of them, showed it in the excessive support of Richard Nixon, even when it became clear he had abused the powers of the Presidency and the integrity of the office. But they said, we have to be loyal to the President. Why? Nothing in the Constitution says that. Nothing that says we need two parties, nothing that says it serves the republic to be overly loyal to a President of your own party.

Second is the idea of the loyal opposition. This has no place except in a parliamentary system. So you can be in opposition for the sake of opposition.

Gerald Ford, when he was before the committee being considered for Vice President, said, "Don't count my record against me." He said he was a member of the opposition and also from Grand Rapids. Now there is nothing in the Constitution that says you have special privileges to be irresponsible if you're from Grand Rapids, even if you're a Republican in the opposition. We've let this thing come in, bipartisan policy, and you say, if it's bipartisan it's good. This is just not so.

I think we've reached the point not only on the substance of the record but as a procedural matter where we have to challenge the two-party operation—I don't call it a system—by which we've been victimized for at least the last twelve years.

Ashmore:

Ambassador Moynihan opened this convocation with a spectacular statement—as all of his pronouncements tend to be. Whatever may be said about his use of rhetoric, the statements by the Ambassador here and elsewhere, supported by statements by the Secretary of State and to some extent by the President, appear to reflect a shift if not in the American formal position with regard to the United Nations, at least in the American attitude toward the U.N.

I'm not aware that this issue has been pursued in any fashion that could be characterized as a public debate on such a fundamental change in U.S. policy toward the U.N. How does that question show up in the Senate, Senator Mansfield? Is it a subject of sustained consideration there? Are we backing off on our commitments or changing our position?

Mansfield:

Well, I think there has been a change. I think that a shift has been occurring for some years now, and the proof can be found in the fact that there has been a reduction in U.S. contributions to various agencies within the United Nations and to the U.N. itself. One reason is that new members of the U.N. can have a population as small as 99,000 and yet be full-fledged members with a vote as strong and as effective as that of the United States and the Soviet Union or the People's Republic of China or any other large country in the General Assembly.

However, while there is a growing dissatisfaction with the U.N. and certainly with its performance of late, with its being manipulated by small countries which make little in the way of contributions but much in the way of rhetoric, I think the Congress still feels inclined towards the U.N.—but not too strongly. And if the situation continues as it has over the past several years I think that there will be a growing disenchantment with the passage of time.

McCarthy:

The actions and words of Ambassador Moynihan are indicative of how we have come to accept that the Ambassador to the United Nations is simply an agent of the executive branch of government; whereas, in fact, he has a double capacity. He's not the Ambassador to the Court of St. James. He represents the United States commitment to the U.N. Charter, which was ratified by the Senate. And he ought to have the sense of his dual capacity.

The early appointments to the U.N. were always former Senators, which was not a bad precedent. They should have stayed with it because the Senator could say, look, I'm the U.N. Ambassador of the President, and I respect him. But I also represent the commitment of the country as it was reflected when the Senate ratified the treaty that established the United Nations.

The U.N. Ambassador is not an ordinary Ambassador, but we've gradually come to accept that he is. Progressively you could see it happening. First, they didn't appoint Senators. That wasn't so bad because they appointed people of some independent status, like Adlai Stevenson and Arthur Goldberg. But even then there was a weakening, as when President Johnson took Goldberg out of the U.N. to settle the Opera strike. That was not really a U.N. function. Mr. Goldberg could have said, look, I must check with the Senate; they may not want me to settle the Opera strike. But he had lost his independence, his two-position strength, by simply saying, I'm the agent of the President. When Nixon began to appoint U.N. Ambassadors, not even the question of independent status or the position of the Ambassadors who might stand against him was taken into account. There was first a career man, which implies no fault to the person, but it was an institutional defect. Then came a newspaper man and then somebody who'd lost an election—they used to make them Postmasters—and now Moynihan.

There was never any conception of the United Nations as something established by an international treaty ratified by the Senate. The U.N. Ambassador doesn't speak only for the Administration. He speaks out of a broader and deeper legal and moral commitment. But we've become so indifferent to institutional relationships that it is like barbarism—a new day every day. It's a question of who occupies Rome at a particular time.

Fraser:

I would like to go back to this question about the statements of Ambassador Moynihan at the U.N. My own judgment is that what he has been saying does not reflect a new American policy posture. The first part of the session this year was the Seventh Special Session, which worked quite well. At the end of it, Ambassador Moynihan made a statement to the effect that this proves that the United Nations can work. The whole experience was a very positive one.

I think what we're finding is an Ambassador who wants to speak in very sharp and tough terms when things happen that he thinks the United States ought to speak out on. And in that respect I think it is more a reflection of his style than a change in a policy position of our government.

With respect to the larger question of the U.N. and Gene McCarthy's description of our representation there, I must say I share some of that same feeling. What I sense is that we don't look at the United Nations as a place of opportunity. I was, for example, especially interested in some of the human rights questions in the U.N. What struck me was that we really hadn't thought of it as a place where we ought to do a lot of early planning and as a place where we could make some advances. We did take some initiatives, but they were started so late that one case, at least, had to be aborted. Within the foreign policy establishment we do not see this as a great opportunity for consultation, for developing of initiatives, and I regret that.

But our problems at the United Nations are not necessarily traceable to that. If there's anything to be said about the U.N. today it's probably that the General Assembly reflects the world as it is; and there it is laid bare before you. And if they do things we don't like, well, that's the way the nations feel about it. I want, however, to underscore the idea that the General Assembly can't do anything that hurts us other than through words, and I don't want to minimize those, because the Zionist Resolution is an example of how words can hurt. They have no power except to assess a budget. The Security Council, where we have a veto, is serving the United States' interests well, however, as is the rest of the U.N. family. So I think we need to be cautious about over-emphasizing the negative side of the U.N.

Baker:

Let me add just a word about the U.N. situation. I want to assure you that as far as I'm concerned, as far as my political-sensing mechanisms go, there is a change in the attitude of the people of the United States toward the U.N. I think it is not, however, that which is often attributed to popular opinion. I do not sense a great demand that we get out of the U.N. I find, as a matter of fact, there's a considerable sentiment toward a stronger position and participation by the United States in the U.N. I find as a matter of fact that by and large the comments to me in Tennessee about the U.N. and those by mail on U.N. subjects generally reflect the attitude that has been adopted by Ambassador Moynihan, that is, stand up and say your piece. I caution against thinking that the United States by and large wants to get out of the U.N. We don't. But we don't want to be run over by it, either. That is my assessment of the current public attitude toward it.

Ashmore:

Senator Baker, I would like to share your optimism on the development of the debate around the central questions of detente and the other foreign policy issues. I hope you turn out to be right. But it seems to me so far that the evidence runs to the contrary. We are in the middle of a presidential campaign, and certainly on the Democratic side it has been going on for a long time. But so far it fits Senator Adlai Stevenson's characterization of the issues conference put on by his own party in Louisville—that it was not a discussion of issues, but a popularity contest, with the outcome determined by an applause meter. This seems to me to be increasingly the case in both parties. So, I wonder about your optimism. When is the debate on the issues going to start?

Baker:

Well, I think it has already started. I think that the very fact that you're having a contest in the Republican primary system between President Ford and former Governor Reagan and that they are at odds on philosophical issues almost guarantees that you have to have a discussion of foreign policy issues. I would urge you to think that the game hasn't really started yet, the opening whistle hasn't been sounded. I have a strong feeling that foreign policy discussion will be one of the major aspects of the presidential campaign in the Republican primary system in 1976.

Anderson:

I happen to think that detente is probably going to be in for a fairly rough time, not just between the two Republican contenders but probably on the other side of the political aisle as well. It is going to come in for rather scathing criticism, and unfortunately not always with a great deal of consistency or with the kind of careful and perceptive analysis that it ought to receive.

McCarthy:

On this question, I don't really know. I don't think detente in itself is going to be much of an issue. You play around with it in sort of high political circles, but there's not much to it as a real issue. With the Chinese, we recognize them in New York, but not in Washington. Somewhere around Havre de Grace is where we meet, and nobody is going to fight on that bridge. As far as Russia is concerned, what we're talking about has really been in the works for a long time.

I don't want to make an issue out of the word, but the realities, as regards the two general areas of detente, seem to me so minimal that if you can get around the word it shouldn't be an issue. I should think almost anyone can come down on the positive side and really not be in any particular political danger.

Audrey Topping:

Senator McCarthy said that we should begin to use our economic power. Also, he implied that military power as it stands today is practically obsolete because it's so powerful it is useless. Now, Senator McCarthy, could you elaborate on that for me, and tell me how could we use our economic power in the same way that we might have used military power. How can we use it in foreign policy?

McCarthy:

Well, I don't know whether we can use it. I hope we wouldn't use it in the way we tried to use the military, but I think it could be a real force. Just take agriculture. We could have used it if we had been producing it up to capacity simply for humanitarian purposes in Bangladesh. We could use it for economic purposes, which in effect is what we're really doing when we sell to Russia. Or we could use it for diplomatic purposes. You could say, look we'll provide you with food under these conditions; and we could also use it as an economic agency. Nobody says, let's use the automobile industry as a diplomatic force. Why not? There's not much force there, but you can argue it. But food is such that we could use it in three respects. We could use it for humanitarian pur-

---

Audrey Topping, who chaired this session, is a photo-journalist, author, and a member of the Board of Trustees, The Fund for Peace.

poses and say, look, we don't care whether it does anything for us economically, or anything for us diplomatically; we're just going to do it because people are starving. But you can also say it will help the balance of payments, and you can also say there are certain circumstances under which we can use food and agriculture and our productivity as a diplomatic force. I would say that's much better than saying we're going to drop bombs.

Anderson:

I wonder if it's quite that simple to equate the use of economic power and military power. Military power as I interpret it serves at least a couple of functions. It can have a deterrent function in which our great might will keep other countries from taking action that you might find inimical to the interests of the United States. Or it can actually be used to wage or prosecute an action, a campaign—a war, if you will. If we try to use economic power in any way to influence the policies of other countries, aren't we going to run the very real risk of being very much resented in the world?

One of my colleagues in the House was going to offer an amendment to the continuing Resolution before us—I think he was finally dissuaded from doing so—that would cut by twenty-five percent the foreign aid that we were giving to any country which voted adversely to us in the United Nations on the anti-Zionist resolution. This was a disastrous proposition if there ever was one. There are clearly some limits to the use of economic power. Obviously we can use our food, we can use something like a Point Four program, economical technical assistance, humanitarian programs of one kind or another. But I think it is oversimplifying to suggest that you can equate the use of our superior economic strength with military power without running the very real risk of incurring some enmity on the part of the other countries of the world.

Question From The Floor:

Why can't we use surplus nuclear weapons to produce energy for the domestic economy?

Anderson:

It is interesting that this question should come up because the Congress is now confronted with making a decision on what do we do about nuclear fuel. How do we increase our present capacity? Dr. Harold Agnew of the Los Alamos laboratory in New Mexico has made the observation that we have sufficient nuclear weapons in our stockpile that we don't need, that some of the fissionable material contained in those weapons could conceivably be diverted to nuclear fuels for peaceful purposes—so it's not a "way out" proposition.

Baker:

Let me make one additional remark about the possibility of mining our weapons stockpile for peaceful fuel purposes. Yes, you can do that. And as a matter of fact, there are some very advanced reactor techniques that lend themselves especially to the utilization of weapons grade material, weapons grade material being in most cases very highly enriched material that is capable of nuclear explosion. There are some very efficient reactors that will utilize that. It also can be used for the detonation of weapons, especially in, say, salt caverns, to produce heat and to gain that heat for the creation of steam and the driving of steam-electric generators. These things all can be done.

But let me caution you about one thing. I'm the senior Republican Senator on the Joint Committee on Atomic Energy. I also represent the state where I guess the largest nuclear installation in the country is located, at

Oak Ridge, Tennessee. And I believe in the future of nuclear power. But one very important caveat must be considered. In my initial remarks, I indicated that I felt one of the most difficult foreign policy problems this country will have to face in years to come is what do we do about the proliferation, not only of nuclear weapons, but also of weapons-grade nuclear material. While there are seven nations now that have or could quickly have explosive devices, there are twelve others that have the demonstrated capability to build explosive devices very promptly. And there are probably an estimated fifty private organizations, corporations, or aggregations of individuals that could do as much.

The question that will confront us in the future, I am convinced, is survival. And survival is going to depend on our ability to cope with this new vector of international force, the possession of extraordinary destructive capacity in the hands not just of the nuclear club of great nations, but of many nations and groups including, possibly, terrorist groups. That genie, nuclear power, is so far out of the bottle that you might as well lay aside any thoughts you have of putting it back. It is going to take every last ounce of resource, of intellect and dedication that we have to find out how to survive into the next generation in the presence of this proliferation of weapons material. But I think we can succeed.

It is going to require the efforts of all nations, of the United Nations, possibly even of new international organizations we have not yet thought of, to do it. It may be that the International Atomic Energy Agency is more important to our future than the U.N. itself. One way or the other, we have to find the answer to that problem because if we don't we'll perish. And the political system in the United States, as we know it, offers us our very best opportunity to realize our ideas about how to do it.

Edward P. Morgan:

On the basis of my own limited knowledge of the electorate—going around as I have been doing in recent months to college campuses—I find them not ready to turn the world off nor wanting to get off, yet at the same time being cynical, being terribly frustrated as to what they can do as members of the electorate. I would like to ask Mr. Anderson, as a Congressman from Illinois—and a distinguished one at that—what do you tell your constituents when they ask you, how can we make you be a better Congressman, or how can we make your opponent or your colleague, Republican or Democrat in the Senate, be better?

Anderson:

Well, I would turn the question around just a little bit and relate an experience I had recently when I was asked to address a business audience on the general topic of how can we best influence the electoral process. And I chose that occasion to suggest to them that what they could best do was to disprove the notion that somehow business was composed merely of an aggregate of special interests and special pleaders who were only interested in such mundane items as whether or not they could deduct expenses for conventions that were held overseas and some other of those things that were purely of parochial concern to their own interests. I suggested that they should lift their eyes to the far horizon and consider some of the changes that were taking place in the world, to see that there was a need for the reconstruction of the economic order.

I suggested they should try to understand that it was no longer, at least in my view, wholly appropriate to think

---

Edward P. Morgan, the former ABC News broadcaster, is a consultant for The Fund for Peace.

in terms of the East-West conflict, not simply because we had replaced that with a detente that was so extraordinarily successful that there was no further danger from the East, but that there was this emerging crisis between North and South. I suggested that they should concern themselves about international issues and the fact that multinational corporations were being challenged around the world on the score of whether or not they were responsible corporate citizens of the countries where they were doing business. I suggested those were the kind of larger issues that would perhaps translate themselves into an improved image of the business community and thereby be an opportunity to be more effective and influential in the electoral process.

I might say also that I found in the college audiences that I have talked to recently that there has been a great deal of interest in the campaign which is being waged now by many groups on the question of doing something about the problem of world hunger. And church communities in my own constituency have stimulated a rather remarkable degree of interest, at least as it is reflected in the mail coming into my office. The fact is that we ought to be doing more as a rich, affluent country than we are presently doing to try to help alleviate the problem of world hunger.

Broadly speaking, what I would suggest in answer to the question is to try to inspire a little bit of that spark of idealism and concern for other parts of the world and other people of the world that I think still burns in the American breast.

Morgan:

Congressman Fraser, you are the head of Americans for Democratic Action and you've been outside of Congress doing things as well as inside. Is my premise valid that there is a gap between the electorate and the elected? And if that is so, how do you close the gap?

Fraser:

I wouldn't have put the problem as a gap between the electorate and the institutions of government. What I have observed is a loss of confidence, an erosion of trust, a loss of confidence in the government to respond. The thing I'm struck by is the number of people who are beginning now to write on the subject, or who are beginning to raise the question of the governability of democracies. The Trilateral Commission had a special group that worked on that subject alone, and one of their main contentions was that there is an overload on the system. They suggested that there has developed in the United States such a large aggregation of various sorts of interests and concerns that the system itself, the governmental system, seems incapable of responding in a way that is satisfactory to this rising level of demands and expectations—that this has led to the drop in confidence.

This is one reason that I hope that in the course of the 1976 election, if there were some way to restore a broader area of consensus, at least in respect to foreign policy, there might be some moderation of the intense demand, and the main thrust of American policy would be rather consistent with the general outlook of the American people. And we would find this part of governance manageable.

This is a thesis that I think is worth noting. Robert Heilbroner wrote in the book *An Inquiry into the Human Prospect* that the problem of the world and the nature of the stresses that are growing—shortages of material, contraction of space and time and increased levels of expectation—all threaten to make governments ungovernable unless they move to more authoritarian modes. His prediction is that over the next century or so there is going to be a rise in authoritarianism in the world.

What I regard as the number one challenge to America is to disprove the inevitability of Heilbroner's thesis, to show that we can, through all of the talents that we have, demonstrate a capacity for self-government to deal with these expectations and demands. And I must say at the moment I think the matter still remains to be resolved.

Baker:

One of the points I tried to make in my initial remarks was that in the final analysis the problem is us. That is, those of us in government imperfectly perceive what the country is trying to tell us. That's an institutional problem which I suspect is with every democracy and has always been with us. But it doesn't make me the slightest bit uneasy about the future of this country or of democracy. I think the problem with politics, and the problem with the responsiveness of the Congress or the adequacy of government, has to do with the level of participation by a sufficient number of people to make sure we're getting an adequate sample of national opinion. I think there is an extraordinary range of competence in the reservoir of collective judgment of the people of the United States. There is but one way to tap that reservoir and that is by direct participation in partisan political activities.

I have a hunch that some statistics I saw the other day may be telling us something, but I'm not yet sure what. They said that in my native state of Tennessee about thirty percent of the people now identify as Democrats and about twenty-two or twenty-three percent identify as Republicans. But almost fifty percent say they could vote for a Republican or Democrat with equal ease, depending on what the candidate had to say. I rather suspect that the two-party system may be under serious attack and that may be the real problem. Because in a way the two-party system in the United States is the fourth department of government. It is the sensing mechanism, the machinery by which you transmit your ideas to the engine and the structure of government. That may be seriously in jeopardy. That is not a permanent problem, I think. We are going to see a rebirth of strong and vital two-party competition beginning in 1976 and for years to come. With Watergate behind us, we are going to see a return to political activism within the usual scope of things.

I also saw in that survey one other statistic I would call to your attention—which I must quickly say did not apply to me. There was a general approval rate in the range of seventy percent for the incumbent federal office holder, but there was also an approval rate of general performance of the federal government of less than forty percent. So the country seemed to be saying, we approve of individual members of Congress or Presidents, but we disapprove of the performance of the government as a whole. And once again, the answer to that, in my judgment, is more broadly based, more active participation in partisan political affairs.

Morgan:

I would like to put a question to Senator Mansfield, relative to the continuing problem between the government and the governed, whether it has to do with communications gap or whatever. Walter Lippmann once told me that the United States was too big to be governed, given the enormous problems that we now have, technological and human, foreign and domestic. Do you agree with that?

Mansfield:

I wouldn't use the word gap, I would use the word differences between the governed and those who govern. I suppose you're referring to the institutions of government, primarily the executive branch and the Congress, when you speak of those who govern, and the people in general when you speak of those who are governed. We know, of course, that the Congress is held in low esteem. I think the latest Harris Poll indicates that we have a standing of about twenty-six percent. The garbage collector has a higher standing than Congress, at least in the polls of the country. But if a Senator or Congressman goes home to his state or his district, he is not held in such low regard. The only answer is that it is the institutions—the institution of the Congress—which the public, the governed, are finding fault with, and they're doing so justifiably. I don't think we've lived up to our responsibility. I think we're afraid to take the steps which must be taken to make sure that we do the best kind of a job for the people whom we supposedly represent.

Congressmen are no longer ambassadors of the people because we're all pretty close, with transportation and communications the way they are today. And I can't blame the people, because the Congress and the Administration have both let them down. What we do is to work at sixes and sevens. We don't come up with conclusions, we don't find solutions. The people, therefore, have a justifiable right to complain. As a result of that, I think there'll be many changes in the next election, and it might not be a bad thing.

REFERENCE MATTER

Speakers and Participants

EQBAL AHMAD, Associate Fellow, Institute for Policy Studies.

JOHN B. ANDERSON, (R.-Ill.), Member, U.S. House of Representatives; Chairman, House Republican Conference.

ROBERT O. ANDERSON, Chairman, Atlantic Richfield Company.

HARRY S. ASHMORE, Associate, Center for the Study of Democratic Institutions; former Editor-in-Chief, Encyclopaedia Britannica.

LES ASPIN, (D.-Wisc.), Member, U.S. House of Representatives; Member, House Committee on Armed Services.

HOWARD H. BAKER, Jr., (R.-Tenn.), U.S. Senator; Co-chairman, Senate Select Committee on Campaign Practices.

RICHARD J. BARNET, Co-founder and Co-director, Institute for Policy Studies; former official, U.S. Arms Controls and Disarmament Agency; former Consultant, Department of Defense.

ELISABETH MANN BORGESE, Associate, Center for the Study of Democratic Institutions; Chairman, (ex officio), International Ocean Institute.

JOHN BRADEMAS, (D.-Ind.), Member, U.S. House of Representatives; Member, House Committee on Education and Labor.

TOM BRADLEY, Mayor of Los Angeles.

FRANK CHURCH, (D.-Idaho), U.S. Senator; Chairman, Senate Select Committee on Intelligence; Member, Committee on Foreign Relations.

BLAIR CLARK, Editor, *The Nation*; former President, *CBS News.*

JOSEPH S. CLARK, former U.S. Senator from Pennsylvania; Chairman, Coalition on National Priorities and Military Policy; Member, Board of Trustees, The Fund for Peace.

INIS L. CLAUDE, Jr., Edward R. Stettinius Professor of Government and Foreign Affairs, University of Virginia, Charlottesville.

RAY S. CLINE, Executive Director of Studies, Georgetown Center for Strategic and International Studies; former Director of Intelligence and Research, Department of State; former Director of Intelligence, Central Intelligence Agency.

WILLIAM COLBY, Director, Central Intelligence Agency.

RANDOLPH P. COMPTON, Chairman, Board of Trustees, The Fund for Peace.

DONALD FRASER, (D.-Minn.), Member, U.S. House of Representatives; Member, United States Delegation to the United Nations.

OTIS GRAHAM, Jr., Associate, Center for the Study of Democratic Institutions; Professor of History, University of California at Santa Barbara.

JAMES P. GRANT, President, Overseas Development Council; former Deputy Assistant Secretary of State.

ROBERTO E. GUYER, United Nations Under Secretary-General for Special Affairs.

MORTON HALPERIN, Director, Project for National Security and Civil Liberties, The Center for National Security Studies of The Fund for Peace; former Deputy Assistant Secretary of Defense.

ROBERT M. HUTCHINS, President, Center for the Study of Democratic Institutions; former President, University of Chicago.

NEIL H. JACOBY, Associate, Center for the Study of Democratic Institutions; Professor, Graduate School of Management, University of California at Los Angeles; former Presidential Economic Advisor.

JACOB K. JAVITS, (R.-N.Y.), U.S. Senator; Member, Senate Foreign Relations Committee.

PHILIP C. JESSUP, former Justice, International Court of Justice; former Professor of International Law, Columbia University.

VERNON E. JORDON, Jr., Executive Director, National Urban League.

GEORGE F. KENNAN, former U.S. Ambassador to the U.S.S.R. and to Yugoslavia.

EDWARD M. KENNEDY, (D.-Mass.), U.S. Senator.

EDWARD LAMB, Member, Board of Trustees, Center for the Study of Democratic Institutions; Chairman, Lamb Enterprises.

GENE R. La ROCQUE, Rear Admiral, U.S.N. (Ret.); Director, Center for Defense Information, The Fund for Peace.

MORRIS L. LEVINSON, Chairman, Executive Committee, Board of Trustees, Center for the Study of Democratic Institutions.

MIKE MANSFIELD, (D.-Mont.), U.S. Senator, Senate Majority Leader.

CARL MARCY, former Staff Director, U.S. Committee on Foreign Relations.

FRANCES McALLISTER, Member, Board of Trustees, Center for the Study of Democratic Institutions.

EUGENE J. McCARTHY, former U.S. Senator from Minnesota.

SEYMOUR MELMAN, Professor of Industrial Engineering, Columbia University.

CHARLES MORGAN, former Executive Director, Washington D.C. office of the American Civil Liberties Union.

EDWARD P. MORGAN, writer and broadcaster.

HANS J. MORGENTHAU, Albert A. Michelson Distinguished Service Professor of Political Science and Modern History Emeritus, University of Chicago.

STEWART R. MOTT, Member, Board of Trustees, The Fund for Peace; Member, Board of Trustees, Center for the Study of Democratic Institutions.

DANIEL P. MOYNIHAN, former U.S. Ambassador to the United Nations.

FRED WARNER NEAL, Associate, Center for the Study of Democratic Institutions. Professor of International Relations and Government, Claremont Graduate School.

ROBERT E. OSGOOD, Dean, School of International Studies, Johns Hopkins University.

GERALD PARSKY, Assistant Secretary of the Treasury for International Affairs.

CLAIBORNE PELL, (D.-R.I.), U.S. Senator; Member, Committee on Foreign Relations.

LORD RITCHIE-CALDER, Labor Member, House of Lords; Associate, Center for the Study of Democratic Institutions.

JAMES R. SCHLESINGER, former United States Secretary of Defense; former Chairman, Atomic Energy Commission.

WILLIAM E. SIMON, Secretary of the Treasury.

MAURICE F. STRONG, Executive Director, U.N. Environment Programme; Member, Advisory Board, The Fund for Peace.

KENNETH W. THOMPSON, Director of Program on Higher Education, International Council on Educational Development; former Vice-President, The Rockefeller Foundation; Member, Advisory Board, The Fund for Peace.

AUDREY R. TOPPING, Photo-journalist and author; Member, Board of Trustees, The Fund for Peace.

RALPH W. TYLER, Vice President, Center for the Study of Democratic Institutions; former Director, The Center for Advanced Study in the Behavioral Sciences.

WILLARD WIRTZ, former Secretary of Labor.

HERBERT R. YORK, Professor of Physics, University of California at San Diego; Science Advisor to Presidents Eisenhower and Kennedy; Associate, Center for the Study of Democratic Institutions.

CHARLES W. YOST, former U.S. Ambassador to the United Nations; Member, Board of Trustees, The Fund for Peace.

ANDREW YOUNG, Member, U.S. House of Representatives; Member, House Rules Committee.

ELMO ZUMWALT, Admiral, U.S.N. (Ret.); former Chief of Naval Operations.

About the Editor

Fred Warner Neal, a Center Associate and professor of International Relations and Government at the Claremont Graduate School, California, holds degrees in Economics and Political Science and was both a Nieman and Littauer Fellow at Harvard. Following war-time service, Mr. Neal became a consultant on Soviet affairs to the State Department and later chief of its division of Foreign Research on Eastern Europe. In 1950, he was a Fulbright Research Scholar at the *Institut de Sciences Politiques* in Paris and in 1961-1962 a Fulbright professor at the universities of Lyons and Strasbourg. A former correspondent for the *Wall Street Journal,* Mr. Neal has dealt extensively with the Soviet Union and Eastern Europe as a naval officer, diplomat and scholar. His most widely-known books are *Titoism in Action; U.S. Foreign Policy and the Soviet Union* (a Center publication); *Yugoslavia and the New Communism; War, Peace and Germany,* and *The Role of Small States in a Big World.* Mr. Neal has been instrumental in organizing the four *Pacem in Terris* Convocations.

The Convocation in Sound

The *Pacem in Terris IV* Convocation, the source for these volumes, was recorded on tape from which a series of 20 audio programs has been edited. The added dimension of sound permits you to experience the excitement of the Convocation almost as if you had been present.

The series includes thirteen major addresses and the seven spirited panel discussions which they sparked. These audiotapes can be used to great advantage in conjunction with the printed volumes, particularly in classrooms and discussion groups.

The programs in this series vary in length from 18 to 81 minutes and are available on cassettes or open reels at 3¾ ips, half track. Prices range from $8.50 to $15.00. For a brochure describing the series in greater detail, please write to: Center Audiotapes, Box 4446, Santa Barbara, California 93103.

The Center for the Study of Democratic Institutions

The Fund for the Republic, Inc.
Box 4068, Santa Barbara, California 93103

 ...ıd for Peace

1855 Broadway, New York, New York 10023

OFFICERS: Randolph P. Compton, *Chairman, Board of Trustees;* Nicholas Nyary, *President;* Abraham Wilson, *Vice President and Counsel;* Stephen R. Paschke, *Treasurer;* Robert W. Gilmore, *Secretary;* Stewart R. Mott, Matthew B. Rosenhaus, *Co-Chairmen, Executive Committee.*

BOARD OF TRUSTEES: Mrs. Marjorie Benton, Arthur D. Berliss, Jr., Cyril E. Black, Julian Bond, William G. Bowen, Edward W. Brooke, Joel I. Brooke, Joseph S. Clark, Barry Commoner, James R. Compton, Randolph P. Compton, Norman Cousins, Morris Dees, Royal H. Durst, Helen Edey, Richard A. Falk, Robert W. Gilmore, G. Sterling Grumman, Charles Guggenheim, Rev. Theodore M. Hesburgh, Harry B. Hollins, Mrs. Thomas E. Irvine, Walter J. Leonard, Joseph P. Lyford, Myres S. McDougal, Howard M. Metzenbaum, The Rt. Rev. Paul Moore, Jr., Stewart R. Mott, Davidson Nicol, Nicholas Nyary, Earl D. Osborn, Augustin H. Parker, Mrs. Maurice Pate, Lawrence S. Phillips, Harvey Picker, Jean Picker, Stanley K. Platt, Albert M. Rosenhaus, Matthew B. Rosenhaus, Alfred P. Slaner, Young M. Smith, Jr., Josephine B. Spencer, Mark Talisman, Audrey R. Topping, Ira D. Wallach, Peter Weiss, Albert Wells, II, Susan W. Weyerhaeuser, Jerome B. Weisner, Harold Willens, Abraham Wilson, Charles W. Yost, Mrs. Arthur M. Young.

PROGRAMS OF THE FUND FOR PEACE

The Center for Defense Information analyzes and reports on defense issues and military spending. *Director,* Rear Admiral Gene R. La Rocque, U.S.N. (Ret.).

The Center for National Security Studies investigates the bearing of measures taken to protect the national security upon constitutional processes and individual citizens' rights. *Director,* Robert L. Borosage.

The Institute for International Policy analyzes American foreign policy, with particular attention to human rights issues and relations with the Third World. *Director,* Donald L. Ranard.

The Institute for the Study of World Politics supports university-based research on issues affecting the prospects for international peace and justice. *Director,* Kenneth W. Thompson.

"In the Public Interest" distributes radio and press commentaries on international issues. *Producer,* Robert A. Maslow; *Principal Commentator,* Edward P. Morgan.